S0-BYF-479

# Bridging the Gap

# Bridging the Gap
## Theory and Practice in Foreign Policy

**Alexander L. George**

Foreword by Ambassador Samuel W. Lewis

UNITED STATES
INSTITUTE OF PEACE PRESS

**Washington, D.C.**

The views expressed in this book are those of the author alone. They do not necessarily reflect views of the United States Institute of Peace.

United States Institute of Peace
1550 M Street, N.W.
Washington, D.C. 20005

© 1993 by Alexander L. George. All rights reserved.

First published 1993

Second printing 1994

Printed in the United States of America

The paper used in this publication meets the minimum requirements of American National Standard for Information Sciences–Permanence of Paper for Printed Library Materials, ANSI Z39.48–1984.

**Library of Congress Cataloging-in-Publication Data**
George, Alexander L.
    Bridging the gap: theory and practice in foreign policy / by Alexander L. George.
        p.    cm.
    ISBN 1–878379–23–2 (alk. paper).—ISBN 1–878379–22–4 (pbk.: alk. paper)
    1. United States—Foreign relations—Iraq.  2. Iraq—Foreign relations—United States.  3. United States—Foreign relations—1981–1989.  4. United States—Foreign relations—1989–1993.  5. Persian Gulf War, 1991—United States.  6. Persian Gulf War, 1991—Causes.  I. United States Institute of Peace.  II. Title.
E183.8.I57G46   1993
327.730567—dc20                                                    92–45232
                                                                        CIP

For
Emil and Irene
and
Lee and Jane

# Contents

# Foreword

Policymakers and scholars alike have long noted the existence of a significant gap between theory and practice in foreign policy. Indeed, some days the distance between the two seems more like a yawning chasm.

One explanation for this gap lies in a conflict between the two different cultures of academe and government. From the standpoint of the policymaker, the scholar is "too academic," all too often prone to abstraction and jargon. The academic can operate in a more relaxed time frame. The policymaker must nearly always act with imperfect information, before a fully satisfactory analysis is complete. He or she does not have the luxury of saying, "Other things being equal . . . " Scholars, on the other hand, may complain that practitioners are too haphazard and ad hoc in their approaches to situations, and too ready to apply pat formulas or supposed lessons of history in uncritical ways. Practitioners place too much faith in intuitive judgment, scholars say, and may make simplistic generalizations.

This gap between theory and practice in foreign policy is a subject that has long interested us at the Institute of Peace, and we have been especially fortunate to have Alexander George with us for the past two years as a distinguished fellow in the Jennings Randolph Program for International Peace.

In this ground-breaking volume, George provides a pene-
trating analysis of the many striking differences between the
two cultures of academia and policymaking. He argues that
while the gap between theoreticians and practitioners cannot
be eliminated, it can be bridged. To that end, he identifies
specific types of "policy-relevant knowledge" needed by the
practitioner, and notes that scholars have not yet provided
adequate conceptualization and general knowledge, drawn
from historical experience, of many strategies and instruments of foreign policy. The lack of such knowledge, he dem-
onstrates, was in part responsible for failures of U.S. policy
towards Iraq in the period leading to the Persian Gulf War.

A point that George stresses is that general knowledge
about a strategy cannot substitute for, but can only aid, the
judgment of the policymaker, who is often called upon
to make difficult choices between competing considerations. Policy-relevant information can play an especially important role during this phase, when the policymaker must
weigh various options while at the same time taking into
account other factors such as the need to muster public support.

But even after you build a bridge, there's no guarantee any-
one will use it. We have a lot of work to do. I say "we" because
it should be a shared responsibility—serious and committed
scholars and those of us in relevant institutional roles need to
work together to promote more meaningful interaction. We
at the Institute of Peace can provide forums and catalytic support. The academic community can provide more of the
policy-relevant knowledge and intellectual frameworks that
are needed. Practitioners can come to the table with an open
mind about better utilizing all the resources available to them.

In particular, we must concentrate on reaching the decisionmakers in ways that can get their attention. Scholars need
to understand better the types of knowledge needed by policymakers, look for ways to disseminate their research more
effectively, and explore ways of conveying its practical impli-

cations to senior policymakers, not just to mid-level analysts. We must together translate theory into practice on the tough new international agenda that lies before our nation. The cause of peacemaking demands nothing less.

Samuel W. Lewis, President
United States Institute of Peace

# Preface

This book addresses the task of bridging the gap between theory and practice in foreign policy. This task requires me to identify the types of knowledge about international relations that will be relevant and useful to those who conduct foreign policy. I have been preoccupied with this challenging task during much of my career, first during the years spent as a member of the RAND Corporation and since 1968 as a member of the Department of Political Science at Stanford University.

I am grateful to the United States Institute of Peace for the award of a Distinguished Fellowship, which enabled me to pursue the project in Washington, D.C., from September 1990 through June 1992. I was delighted to find that the Institute shares a keen interest in developing scholarly knowledge for use in policymaking and works in constructive ways to encourage two-way interaction between academic scholars and policy specialists.

My study has turned out to be somewhat different, and I think better, for having been pursued in the stimulating environment of Washington. Closer proximity to the policy world forced me to reexamine and sharpen some of the ideas I entertained in the past. I believe I have a better understanding now, which I have tried to communicate in this book, of the kinds of knowledge needed in policymaking and how such knowledge, when it is available, can contribute to policymaking.

More important, the preparation of the study and in particular the chapters that assess the strategies the United States has employed toward Iraq since 1988 strongly confirmed a long-standing concern that the state of existing policy-relevant knowledge is inadequate and that much additional scholarly research directed to producing such knowledge is badly needed.

I was fortunate in preparing the study to have had the opportunity to discuss U.S. policies toward Iraq with ten senior policy officials in the State Department, the Department of Defense, and the staff of the National Security Council. These individuals participated in and are knowledgeable about U.S. policy toward Iraq. They kindly read and commented on earlier drafts of chapters in part two of the study. I asked these policy specialists to tell me whether I had correctly stated the facts and whether my analytical interpretations of U.S. policy toward Iraq were reasonable. Their responses to these questions were generally reassuring, and they offered additional information and useful judgments, which I have attempted to incorporate into these chapters. For understandable reasons, these officials—two no longer in the government—preferred to remain anonymous.

I am indebted to Jane Holl, a specialist on war termination problems, for helpful comments on earlier drafts of chapter 8 and for allowing me to see several as yet unpublished essays on this topic. I benefited also from stimulating conversations with many foreign policy specialists who are not in the government, though many of them previously were. Some of them kindly read and commented on earlier drafts of some of the chapters in the book. In alphabetical order they are Sanjoy Banerjee, Andrew Bennett, Robert Bowie, Dan Caldwell, Arthur Cohen, Eliot Cohen, Chester Crocker, Terry Deibel, Hugh DeSantis, Daniel Druckman, Arun Elhance,

Muhammad Faour, Juliette George, Ashraf Ghani, Richard Herrmann, Mark Hoffman, Stephen Hosmer, Fred Iklé, Martin Indyk, Bruce Jentleson, Robert Jervis, Michael Krepon, Steven Kull, James Laue, Joseph Lepgold, Samuel Lewis, David Little, Sean Lynn-Jones, Michael Mandelbaum, Ernest May, Alexander Moens, Joseph Montville, Patrick Morgan, Joseph Nye, Robert Pastor, Don Peretz, Alan Platt, Jerrold Post, William Quandt, Stephen Rock, Walt Rostow, Robert Rothstein, Shimon Shamir, William Simons, Richard Smoke, Louis Sohn, Janice Gross Stein, Stephen Stedman, Eric Stern, and I. William Zartman. If they read this book, I trust they will see reflected in it some of their observations and suggestions.

I wish to express appreciation to Samuel Lewis, president of the Institute, and Michael Lund, director of the Jennings Randolph fellowship program, for their unflagging encouragement of the project and insightful suggestions for improving the study. I also wish to thank Otto Koester and Joseph Klaits, program officers, and Barbara Cullicott, program administrator, for providing so supportive and congenial an environment for serious research; Dan Snodderly for his good-humored and incisive editorial suggestions; Blaine Vesely and Denise Dowdell for indispensable and efficient library services; Mia Cunningham for her careful copyediting; and Anne Cushman, Tarak Barkawi, and William Tanzola for their competent and cheerful research and secretarial services. Finally, as so often in the past, my wife, Juliette, provided indispensable support and understanding as well as insightful suggestions and comments.

# Introduction

The central purpose of this study is to encourage better communication and closer collaboration between academic scholars who study foreign policy and practitioners who conduct it. Better communication requires a better understanding by both scholars and practitioners of the three types of knowledge needed in policymaking. In addition to reliable and timely intelligence about situational developments, policymakers need (1) *conceptualization of strategies*—a conceptual framework for each of the many different strategies and instruments available to them for attempting to influence other states. Policymakers also need (2) *general, or generic, knowledge* of each strategy, based on study of past experience that identifies the uses and limitations of each strategy and the conditions on which its effective employment depends. Finally, policymakers need a sophisticated, insightful understanding of each of the state-actors with whom they interact—what I shall refer to as (3) *actor-specific behavioral models*—in lieu of a dangerous tendency to assume that they can be regarded as rational, unitary actors.

These three types of knowledge are discussed in great detail in this study to make the following points:

- Policymakers often operate with inadequate knowledge or erroneous assumptions or both regarding the strategies they seek to employ in the conduct of foreign policy.
- Conceptualization and general knowledge of many foreign policy strategies and actor-specific models are inadequate in important respects and as yet poorly developed.
- Much additional scholarly research in academic centers and within the government is needed to improve the knowledge base for foreign policy.

Many policy specialists have a strong aversion to the idea that theory can have relevance and potential utility for policymaking. In fact, as many scholars have discovered, the eyes of practitioners often glaze over at the first mention of the word "theory" in conversation. I have no desire in this study to convert policymakers into adherents of theory; in fact, I shall point out in some detail the weakness of academic theories of international relations from the perspective of the types of knowledge needed in policymaking. However, it must also be said that good theories provide relevant and useful conceptual frameworks by means of which to understand the general requirements of a strategy and the general logic associated with its effective employment. Such theoretical-conceptual knowledge is critical for policymaking. And, as a matter of fact, all policymakers make use of some such theory and conceptual frameworks, whether consciously or not. That is, in employing a strategy, policymakers rely on assumptions, often tacit assumptions, about the strategy's general requirements and logic. The gap between theory and practice that forms the starting point for this study is not in policymakers' non-use of theoretical concepts, but in the failure to analyze them more critically and to be more aware of the impact of theoretical-conceptual assumptions on policymaking.

I have discovered in my conversations with policy specialists that if I avoid the word "theory" and speak instead of "generic knowledge" about foreign policy, they are much more receptive to the relevance of "generic knowledge" for policymaking. I believe this is so partly because policy specialists recognize that generic problems exist in the conduct of foreign policy—for example, that the task of deterrence emerges repeatedly over time and with different adversaries. Therefore, policy specialists readily agree that general, or generic, knowledge about the uses and limitations of a particular strategy, derived from study of past experience, could be very helpful when strategy must be used in a new situation. Incidentally, whether the empirical generalizations that comprise generic knowledge should also be regarded as a form of theory—or "laws," as some scholars prefer to call this type of knowledge—should not get in the way of recognizing the importance of generic knowledge for policymaking.

I have chosen to demonstrate the importance and relevance of all three types of knowledge in part two of this study in a very concrete manner by calling attention to the weak knowledge base that underlay five of the six strategies the United States pursued toward Iraq in 1988–91 and that contributed to their ineffectiveness.

The reader will want to know why I speak in the title of this book of "bridging" the gap rather than "eliminating" it. The choice of words is deliberate and of considerable importance. I will argue that the gap between the three types of knowledge I have identified (which can be very loosely referred to as policy-relevant theory) and practice can be only bridged and not eliminated. Scholarly knowledge of this kind can have only an indirect and often limited impact on policymaking. Since I also claim that the contribution of these three types of knowledge is often critical for sound policy nevertheless, I need to explain this apparent contradiction.

The types of knowledge identified in this study serve as inputs to policy analysis within the government and as aids to the judgment of policymakers. Such knowledge cannot substitute for policy analysis or for the policymaker's judgment.

Even the best conceptualization of a given foreign policy strategy and the most highly developed general knowledge of that strategy cannot substitute for competent policy analysis within the government, in which analysts must consider whether some version of that strategy is likely to be viable in the particular situation at hand. Similarly, such knowledge cannot substitute for the judgment policymakers must exercise in deciding whether to employ the strategy on a given occasion, since that judgment takes into account other relevant considerations not encompassed by general knowledge of the strategy. It is in this sense that scholarly knowledge has an indirect and often limited impact on policy. It is important that we understand why this is so, and this question is addressed particularly in chapters 2 and 10.

How, then, can policy-relevant knowledge aid policy analysis and the policymaker's judgment? First, it can assist in making a sound diagnosis of a problem situation; second, it can help identify an effective policy response for dealing with that problem. Thus, policy-relevant knowledge contributes to two essential functions in policymaking: the diagnostic task and the prescriptive one. I place particular emphasis on the diagnostic contribution policy-relevant theory and knowledge are capable of making than to their ability to prescribe sound choices of policy. Correct diagnosis of a policy problem and of the context in which it occurs should precede and—as in medical practice—is usually a prerequisite for efforts to make the best choice from among treatment options. The analogy with the medical profession is an apt one, since the policymaker, like the physician, acts as a clinician in striving to make a correct diagnosis of a problem before determining how best to prescribe for it.

* * * *

It may be useful in this introduction to recall the origins, background, and framework of this study. In 1966, while still a member of the RAND Corporation, I saw the need to supplement efforts to formulate general theories of international relations with theories that are more relevant for the conduct of foreign policy. To this end I initiated a small research project, "Theory and Practice in International Relations." Later, upon moving to Stanford University in 1968, I elaborated the title to "Bridging the Gap between Theory and Practice in Foreign Policy," and this topic has remained the focus of my research program and, in one way or another, of most of my studies since then.

Quite early in implementing this research program I concluded that it would be necessary to move beyond structural realist theory, rational choice theory, and game theory approaches that were (and are still) favored and being pursued by many talented scholars. These deductive approaches to theory development "black-box" both the process of policymaking and strategic interaction between states; that is, they deal with these processes by assumption. Instead, I felt it necessary to engage in direct but admittedly difficult empirical study of policymaking processes and strategic interaction between actors. However, I do not regard deductive and empirical ways of approaching the task of developing international relations theory as antithetical. Rather, like many other researchers, I believe the development of both deductive and empirical approaches to theory development can be improved by trying to link them more closely. Finally, the reader should keep in mind that I use the word *theory* to encompass a broad range of ways of formulating knowledge that come out of the scholarly tradition.

I found it useful in developing policy-relevant theory, which I regard as the type of knowledge needed for what historians used to refer to as statecraft, to distinguish between two types of theory. *Substantive theory*, the first type, deals with standard foreign policy undertakings and strategies such as deterrence, crisis management, coercive diplomacy, détente, war termination, mediation and dispute resolution, and security cooperation. In selecting some of these foreign policy activities for systematic study, I was motivated by historical events that led me to believe that U.S. leaders needed a better knowledge base from which to manage Cold War crises so as to avoid war. My interest in studying deterrence, for example, was aroused by the outbreak in June 1950 of the Korean War, which I regarded as a conflict that could have been avoided. Similarly, what seemed to me another avoidable war later that year in Korea—this time with the People's Republic of China—aroused my interest in better understanding the requirements and modalities of crisis management. Later, again reacting to what I regarded as a misguided, flawed American policy, I began to study the limitations of coercive diplomacy after observing the abortive U.S. effort to use air power in early 1965 to intimidate North Vietnam. Some years later, I initiated a large collaborative study to try to gain insight into why U.S.-Soviet efforts to cooperate on security issues since the end of World War II sometimes succeeded and, on other occasions, failed. And more recently, I focused together with others on trying to understand the phenomenon of inadvertent war, that is, a war that occurs although at the beginning of a diplomatic crisis neither side wants or expects war.

*Process theory,* the second type of theory, on the other hand, focuses on how to structure and manage the policymaking process in ways that will improve information processing and foster sound judgments, thus increasing the likelihood of better policy decisions. My research on these matters was stimulated by studies that pointed to various malfunctions of the U.S. policymaking system that often lowered the quality of policy decisions. My conception of the contribution that process theory should make to improving the quality of policy decisions is a broad one. It rejects placing exclusive reliance on the criterion of *technical rationality* as a basis for arriving at high-quality policy decisions and emphasizes that the policymaking process needs to be sensitive as well to the broader criterion of *value rationality* and to normative consid-erations.[1]

Both substantive theory and process theory have important contributions to make to the improvement of foreign policy. Quite obviously, substantive knowledge of foreign affairs can have no impact on policy unless it enters into the process of policymaking. Substantive knowledge must combine with the effective structuring and management of the policymaking process in order to improve the analytic (versus the political) component of policymaking.

The present study deals almost exclusively with substantive theory and the knowledge requirements of foreign policy. However, I have included in chapter 2 a realistic, even sober, view of some aspects of the policymaking process that tend to crowd out or reduce the impact of substantive knowledge. It is important for scholars who are interested in developing policy-relevant knowledge not to overintellectualize policy-making by assuming that it is or should be devoted exclu-sively to identifying and choosing high-quality policy options based on the criterion of analytic rationality.

\* \* \* \*

The present study addresses only some of the substantive knowledge requirements needed for the conduct of foreign policy. Not included are a host of important problems that affect the interests of individual nations and their peoples, to which policy specialists must be attentive. Among these prob-lems are proliferation of nuclear weapons and other mass de-struction capabilities, environmental and ecological prob-lems, population and demographic trends, problems of food production and distribution, water scarcities, sanitation and health problems, and emergence of nationalistic, ethnic, and religious conflicts. Well-informed, objective analyses of these problems are an essential part of the knowledge require-ments for conduct of foreign policy.

Scholars can make a number of other contributions to policymaking that will not be taken up in the present study but
that should at least be briefly noted. Among these are the col-
lection and orderly presentation of a variety of data and the
identification of trends regarding many different aspects of
the international system. Scholars also perform a useful, indeed a necessary, task by developing better concepts and conceptual frameworks, which should assist policymakers in ori-
enting themselves to the phenomena and the problems with
which they must deal. Finally, although scholars may not be
in a good position to advise policymakers how best to deal
with a specific instance of a general problem that requires
urgent and timely action, they can often provide a useful,
broader discussion of how to think about and understand
that general problem—such as, for example, the problem of
ethnicity and nationalism.

The present study focuses on a different kind of substantive knowledge that is needed by policymakers for conducting relations with other states. This is the type of knowledge
needed for what diplomatic historians used to refer to as
statecraft. From this standpoint the essential task of foreign
policy is to develop and manage relationships with other
states in ways that will protect and enhance one's own security
and welfare. This objective requires that policymakers clearly
define their own state's interests, differentiate these interests
in terms of relative importance, and make prudent judgments as to acceptable costs and risks of pursuing them. (Admittedly, these fundamental tasks of policymaking are often
not easily accomplished.) Policymakers must identify, analyze, and deal with conflicts of interest with other states.
When an accommodation of their conflicting interests is not
possible, policymakers must try to narrow and manage the
disputed issues in ways that reduce the potential for destructive conflicts and contamination of the entire relationship. At
the same time, the development and management of relationships with other states requires leaders to recognize and

seek out common interests and to develop policies for pro-
moting them. Statecraft includes strategies for cooperation
and the building of institutions and regimes as well as for
conflict avoidance, management, and resolution.

The realist theory of international relations offers some important guidelines for the practice of statecraft. Realist
theory is not a theory of foreign policy, however (see chapter 9), and it provides very little of the substantive knowledge
needed for the practice of statecraft. Thus, in addition to the
help policymakers get from realist theory, they require sophisticated conceptualization of the many different instruments of foreign policy and the various strategies that can be
employed to influence other states. In addition, they need
general knowledge of the uses and limitations of each policy
instrument and strategy. This type of general, or generic,
knowledge is most useful to policymakers when it is couched
in the form of *conditional generalizations;* conditional generalizations identify (1) the conditions that favor successful use of
each particular instrument and strategy, and (2) other conditions that make success very unlikely.

Realist theory itself provides neither conceptualization nor
generic knowledge of the many policy instruments and strategies. Another limitation of realist theory is that it assumes
that all states can be treated as rational, unitary actors. The
conduct of foreign policy, however, requires differentiated
knowledge of each adversary, ally, or neutral state with which
one is interacting. Therefore, the realist model must be substantially supplemented if not altogether replaced by a discriminating actor-specific model.

These three types of knowledge—conceptualization of
strategies, generic knowledge, and actor-specific models—
and their role in policymaking are discussed in detail in
chapter 10.

Earlier I indicated that the present study focuses on strategies and instruments of policy. However, I will not undertake the ambitious task of discussing the state of existing

knowledge of all of the many policy instruments and strategies that states employ in interacting with each other. Instead,
I will focus attention in part two on a smaller number of strategies and use them to illustrate the general points I wish to
make about the need for policy-relevant knowledge.

\* \* \* \*

This study is addressed to two types of readers: those whose
primary orientation derives from participation in the world
of scholarship, whether primarily in academic settings or
elsewhere, and those whose orientation to foreign policy has
been largely influenced by having participated in the policymaking process. Accordingly, I have tried to write this book
in a way that will be understood both by policy specialists and
by academic scholars. In addressing complex and difficult issues I have tried to minimize use of abstract jargon and have
made minimal use of footnotes and references.

Bridging the gap between the theory and practice of foreign policy requires in a very real sense bridging the differences between the two cultures of academia and the policymaking world. It is important to recognize and be sensitive to
these two cultures if we are to make further progress in developing policy-relevant knowledge. This task, however difficult, is by no means insurmountable. I believe that a start can
be made by focusing in chapter 1 on the relationship between
knowledge and action, a problem that should engage the interest of both scholars and policy specialists. Three questions
are posed: (1) What contributions can knowledge make to
policymaking? (2) What types of knowledge are most relevant
for policy? (3) How can this type of knowledge be developed
by scholars and research specialists and how can it be employed effectively by policymakers?

Part One

# The Gap between Knowledge and Action

# 1. The Two Cultures of Academia and Policymaking

> The policymaker, unlike an academic analyst, can rarely wait until all the facts are in. . . . He is very often under strong pressure to do something, to take some action. . . . The capacity of human beings to deal with situations of vast complexity is very limited. The human mind needs a highly simplified "map" of a situation if it is going to be capable of taking any action or making a decision.—Robert Bowie[1]

The development of theory about international relations by academic scholars and the use of this knowledge by practitioners in the conduct of foreign policy have been handicapped by the different cultures in which they have traditionally resided.[2] Members of these two communities have been socialized in quite different professional and intellectual worlds. They generally define their interest in the subject of international relations differently. The policymaker is typically preoccupied with how best to promote the national interest of the United States. However, many scholars believe this to be too narrow an approach to international relations and choose to work with a set of values broader than those encompassed by conventional notions of the national interest. An additional obstacle to bridging the two cultures is the

3

reluctance of some scholars, particularly when they disagree with the government's foreign policies, to serve as "technicians" for the state by providing specialized knowledge that may be "misused." Such scholars prefer the roles of critic and "unattached intellectual."[3]

With the passage of time, however, the gulf between the two communities has eroded substantially. As academic scholars and academically trained specialists in international affairs have moved in and out of government service, and as former foreign policy practitioners have found places in academia, a substantial intermingling of the two cultures has taken place. Many policy specialists and technical experts holding positions in the policymaking hierarchy, especially in middle levels, have had advanced training in international relations or in related fields. In addition to drawing on their own familiarity with scholarly knowledge, they are likely to maintain contact with academic scholars and their publications. These policy specialists can thereby serve as an informal bridge between the two worlds and increase the likelihood that relevant scholarly knowledge can be used in policymaking. Policy specialists in the government increasingly have tried in a variety of ways to tap and make use of the knowledge of scholars on specific policy problems. Frequently used for this purpose are conferences and meetings at which academic specialists meet with policy specialists to discuss a particular problem. Foundations have made important contributions in encouraging interaction between academics and policy specialists; for example, the Council on Foreign Affairs has for many years conducted a fellowship program that places carefully selected young international relations scholars in the government for a year and mid-career policy specialists in academic centers of foreign policy and security research. As a result, progress is being made in understanding how scholarly research on international relations can benefit from the perspective and experience of the policy world and how, in turn, policymaking can benefit from scholarly research. The objective of the present study is to further this development.

This favorable trend, however, remains quite uneven. For example, the rapidity with which academic and policymaking perspectives converged after World War II in the field of strategic studies and arms control was quite striking. Because the field was relatively new and wide open it attracted the thoughtful interest of a number of academic scholars who had been exposed to problems of military strategy and operations during the war and who were galvanized by the new challenge of understanding the impact of nuclear weapons on strategy and foreign policy. In fact, much of the impetus and some of the most important early contributions to the new field of strategic studies and arms control came from civilians such as Bernard Brodie, William Kaufmann, and Herman Kahn and from members of the new postwar think tanks such as the RAND Corporation. International law appears to be another subfield of international relations in which there has been good two-way communication between government specialists and academic scholars. And the infusion of economists into government departments concerned with foreign policy may have brought the academic and policymaking perspectives closer together in related issue areas.

On the other hand, progress in bridging the worlds of policymaking and academia has been much slower and more difficult in regard to the role of force and threats of force in the conduct of diplomacy and in regard to the various dimensions of conflict management. And though there are striking exceptions, even less appears to have been accomplished in bringing about a more fruitful, sustained interplay between academic scholars and practitioners in the important issue areas of conflict avoidance and conflict resolution, and more generally in the study of international cooperation and long-term change in the international system.

The intermingling of scholars and practitioners in both worlds offers important opportunities for learning how to make additional progress in bridging the gap between the two cultures and their traditional perspectives. It is just this opportunity and challenge that has motivated the present study. It is well to begin by clearing some of the underbrush that still stands in the way and formulating a common ground on which productive two-way interaction can take place between the theoretical approach to study of international relations pursued in academia and the practitioner's need for the kind of knowledge that can facilitate formulation of sounder, more effective policy. That common ground, it will be suggested here, is to be found in the relationship between knowledge and action.

In the following sections I shall consider some typical reservations, which may or may not be wholly justified, that many (though not all) practitioners of foreign policy and many (though not all) academic international relations scholars have about their respective approaches to the subject.[4] I hope the reader will keep in mind that this is a highly condensed characterization and that there is considerable variation in the views held by members of both groups. In part three, I offer a different set of observations regarding how the relationship between knowledge and action can be conceptualized so as to provide a bridge between scholars, who specialize in the production of better knowledge of international relations, and government policy specialists, whose responsibility includes using general knowledge to help top policymakers make their decisions.

## Practitioners' Reservations about Academic Theory

Academic specialists have often been struck by the fact that the eyes of policy specialists quickly glaze over at the first mention of the word "theory" or the phrase "scientific study of international relations." This reaction is unsettling to academic scholars, for they have been socialized in a world in which the development of theory and scientific knowledge enjoys the greatest respect and highest priority.

What lies behind this glazing over of the practitioners' eyes? It is a certain image of academic efforts to theorize about international relations and policymaking. A familiar complaint is that academic scholars do not understand how policy is actually made, even when they undertake in case studies to follow the paper trail of a particular decision. Lacking an understanding of the process, academics tend to over-intellectualize policymaking and exaggerate the importance of analytic rationality as the criterion on the basis of which policy is, or at least ought to be, chosen (see chapter 2).

Practitioners and policy specialists also question the high level of abstraction often employed in scholarly writings, and they are dubious about the relevance and utility of many of the theoretical generalizations and models put forward by academic researchers.

Even when the results of scholarly research are recognized as potentially relevant, they are often under-used for another reason: not a few policy specialists exposed to the scholarly literature have concluded that most university professors seem to write largely for one another and have little inclination or ability to communicate their knowledge in terms comprehensible to policymakers. Some practitioners are acutely uncomfortable with the unfamiliar and, to them, pretentious jargon with which their activities are described, and they are perplexed by the esoteric explanations that are given for their behavior. One may recall in this connection Secretary of State Dean Acheson's tongue-in-cheek response when he became aware of the way his role in the U.S. decision of June 1950 to come to the assistance of South Korea had been referred to in a scholarly study. Acheson took exception to being treated as a "dependent variable" in that study, observing dryly that he thought it obvious that he had played the role of an "independent variable" in that crisis.

Practitioners also object to what they consider a heroic but misguided effort by academicians to put foreign policy on a scientific basis. Insisting that statecraft is an art and not a science, practitioners emphasize the role of judgment in making policy decisions. (I return to what "judgment" encompasses in chapter 2.) Some years ago George Ball, then under secretary of state, emphasized this point in describing the complexity of the problem he and his colleagues had faced during the Cuban missile crisis: "We were presented . . . with an equation of compound variables and multiple unknowns. No one has yet devised a computer that will digest such raw data as was available to us and promptly print out a recommended course of action. . . ."[5] And other former policymakers have also emphasized that the president, unlike the academic scholar, has to make a decision in which *all* the variables are at play; the scholar deliberately limits the number of variables considered in order to develop a parsimonious theory.

How do policy specialists respond to quantitative studies that attempt to account for war and other foreign policy outcomes by means of statistical correlations? Quantitative studies may claim, for example, to "account for" (but not necessarily explain) 75 percent of the variance in the outcome of many instances of a particular phenomenon. Such studies may provide policymakers with a useful indication of the probability distribution, but of course this finding does not tell whether an actual case falls in that group or is among the 25 percent that are *not* accounted for. A more important dissatisfaction with this type of study among policymakers stems from the fact that it typically ignores domestic political and decision-making variables. The policy relevance of such studies is limited, therefore, because they do not include variables over which policymakers have some leverage that they can use to try to influence outcomes. Therefore, such studies give policymakers no help in deciding what they can do to avoid unwanted outcomes and to achieve desired ones.

More generally, the gap between academic scholars and

practitioners reflects the difference between their professional missions. Academics aim at increasing general knowledge and wisdom about international relations; practitioners
are more interested in the type of knowledge that increases
their ability to influence and control the course of events. In
the role of policymaker, individuals often adapt by becoming
action oriented: they need uncomplicated diagnoses and solutions in order to take action. It is not surprising that policy
specialists should "want short, precise answers to problems
rapidly. . . . But the academic cannot give a short answer to a
policymaker's question—not because the academic is long-
winded or pretentious, but because [it appears to him that]
that the short answer is in fact not an answer. . . ."[6]

Similarly, practitioners find it difficult to make much use of
academic approaches such as structural realist theory and
game theory, which assume that all state actors are alike and
can be expected to behave in the same way in given situations,
and which rest on the simple, uncomplicated assumption
that states can be regarded as rational unitary actors. On the
contrary, practitioners believe they need to work with actor-
specific models (see chapter 10) that grasp the different internal structures and behavioral patterns of each state and
leader with which they must deal. Similarly, although practitioners can accept the academician's argument that the assumption of pure rationality is a powerful tool for the con-
struction of theory, they are more impressed with the caveat
that sophisticated academicians add, namely, that the validity of such theories of course must be established by empirical research that examines the "fit" between the theory and
reality.

Practitioners have a similar reservation when encouraged
to use new psychological theories, developed under carefully
controlled laboratory conditions, that purport to—and indeed do—have relevance for some aspects of foreign policy.
Perhaps drawing on their memories of undergraduate psychology courses, policy specialists recall that experimental

psychologists themselves emphasize that theories developed under laboratory conditions may or may not have external validity in real-world situations.

Policy specialists also believe that there are often good reasons to question the results of academic studies that explain and evaluate foreign policy decisions. Policymakers suspect that scholarly studies are not always as objective as they appear, and that they contain political or ideological biases. Given the proliferation of competitive "advocacy analysis" in the ever-expanding world of think tanks and academic centers, policymakers can find excuses and justification for rejecting those studies that do not fit their own policy orientations and rely instead on those that do.

Then, too, the data base used in scholarly studies, policy specialists argue, is often inadequate and can distort the scholar's interpretations. Not only is access to classified information for such studies limited, but available declassified information does not give the whole picture and may introduce flaws in the interpretations. Similarly, data obtained from current or former policymakers are subject to a variety of limitations that scholars are often unaware of or do not adequately take into account. In some cases scholars rely too uncritically on information about unsuccessful policies provided by lower level policy specialists who say in effect, "We had the correct analysis of the problem and the right answer, but the higher-ups didn't listen."

Finally, the practitioner is often wary of academic research theories and generalizations that purport to provide policy advice. A strong reservation of this kind was expressed by Richard Goodwin, a former policy adviser in the Kennedy and Johnson administrations, in a sharply critical review some years ago of the book *Arms and Influence*, written by Thomas Schelling, a leading strategic theorist.[7] For Goodwin, Schelling's book "raises troubling questions about the growing body of social-science literature devoted to military theory." Goodwin rejected the view that what Schelling called "the diplomacy of violence" can be the subject of systematic theory, and he marshaled several familiar arguments to buttress his conclusion. For Goodwin, history is sui generis, and to generalize from one historical crisis to another is therefore dangerous and "almost guarantees error." In any case, the task of developing valid generalizations is, according to Goodwin, virtually insuperable. And even if some sort of generalization were somehow derived, its relevance to any immediate policy problem could not be determined, since in almost any situation policymakers must act without knowing all the facts, and the variables in the situation "are so numerous that they elude analysis." These concerns led Goodwin to put forward a sober warning: "The most profound objection to this kind of strategic theory is not its limited usefulness but its danger, for it can lead us to believe we have an understanding of events and a control over their flow which we do not have." I shall return to Goodwin's concern later in this chapter.

## Academic Scholars' Reservations about the Policy World

Although specialists in the study of international relations sharply disagree among themselves over questions of method and theory, many of them hold the belief that policymakers are too aconceptual and atheoretical, even anticonceptual and antitheoretical. At the same time, academic scholars note that policymakers and their advisers often do operate with a general view of international politics influenced by their acquaintance with realist theory and such related concepts as national interest and balance of power. Academic specialists express concern, however, that the realist theory that shapes the mind-set of these policymakers is a warmed-over and simplified version of Hans Morgenthau's influential post–World War II textbook *Politics Among Nations* and similar efforts by others in that era to steer American foreign policy away from what they considered to be a well-meaning but naively idealist orientation. These academic scholars hope that policymakers do not take at face value Morgenthau's dubious contentions that power is and ought to be the dominant objective of foreign policy; that the national interest is an objective, scientific criterion that can provide policymakers with firm guidance in choosing policies; and that ideology is merely rhetorical justification for policy and does not (and should not) play any role in determining national policy. Elements of this earlier classical realist theory have been criticized and reformulated by a new generation of academic scholars.

The simplified and dated view of realist theory employed by many policymakers is seen by academics as part of a larger problem. Granted that policy specialists and top policymakers come into government with intellectual capital derived from earlier education and other relevant experience, their work in government provides most of them with little opportunity for replenishing and updating their knowledge. Full-time work in government offers inadequate opportunity and stimulates little inclination for keeping abreast of relevant scholarly knowledge. More than one policymaker has expressed concern that one eventually uses up and exhausts one's intellectual capital.[8] Academic scholars find that policy professionals tend to have a fixed body of knowledge that is relatively impervious to outside influence and challenge. Commenting on this state of affairs, some scholars who have had opportunities to participate in and observe policymaking speak of the policy professionals' resistance to knowing what they do not already know.

Academics are skeptical of claims that the intuitive judgment and experience of policy specialists suffice to ensure sound foreign policy decisions, that they need not make use of what academics refer to as theory and systematic empirical knowledge regarding the uses and limitations of the various instruments of statecraft. Academics also point out that in fact, whether policymakers realize it or not, they do use theory, though usually in the form of a variety of implicit assumptions, beliefs, and maxims that are seldom raised to full consciousness and examined critically.[9] Policy beliefs and maxims of this kind emerge from an individual's personal or vicarious experience of past historical events, and from lessons passed on from earlier generations of policymakers. Such policy beliefs and historical analogies are usually rather simple, uncomplicated formulations of causal relationships. An example is the familiar proposition derived from the experience of the 1930s that was and remains influential in shaping American policy, namely, "If appeasement, then World War III," or, as it is often worded, "If we appease the opponent now we shall have to fight a much larger war against him later."

To the academician, simple generalizations of this kind seriously oversimplify the complexity of foreign policy strategies and outcomes. They should be replaced by *conditional generalizations;* thus, one needs to ask *"Under what conditions* is appeasement counterproductive and serves to increase the likelihood of war?" But the question should also be asked, *"Under what different conditions* is appeasement a useful, viable strategy for conflict resolution?" (The strategy of appeasement is discussed in chapter 5.) Systematic study of a variety of historical cases and more thoughtful reflection, the academician argues, are needed to provide discriminating conditional generalizations of this kind.[10] (At the same time, however, it must be said, academic scholars have yet to produce a systematic, empirically grounded, and differentiated theory of appeasement.)

A related criticism singles out the policymaker's habit of relying on and often misusing a single historical precedent or analogy.[11] Policymakers and scholars who agree with Richard Goodwin maintain that history is sui generis and that each case is unique; nonetheless, in practice they often search for and use historical analogies to help them deal with their "unique" cases. Academicians see policy specialists as uninterested in cumulating lessons from a number of different historical cases and having no effective method for doing so. As a result, or so academicians believe, policymakers often do not take into account and digest a broad variety of relevant historical experience, and therefore what they do learn from history is of dubious validity.

For these and other reasons, academic scholars believe policymakers need to develop a better understanding of how their own beliefs and tacit assumptions about the international system, international politics, and other actors in the state system influence their perception of developments, their diagnoses of situations, and their judgments. Academics are therefore very much in agreement with the observation made many years ago by a former State Department planner, Louis Halle, that the foreign policy of a nation addresses itself not to the external world per se but rather to "the *image* of the external world" that is in the minds of those who make foreign policy. Halle concluded his book on American foreign policy with a sober warning: "In the degree that the image is false, actually and philosophically false, no technicians, however proficient, can make the policy that is based on it sound."[12] Accordingly, academic specialists suggest, practitioners should recognize the importance of subjecting the operative beliefs and policy maxims they rely upon to scrutiny via scholarly studies of a broader range of historical experience.

Finally, academic specialists believe that in choosing a policy, policymakers are too often swayed by political considerations rather than by the results of objective analysis. According to this view, policymakers are less inclined to choose the best policy than to choose one that commands greater political support and avoids too much controversy. Another criticism is that even when good policies are announced, the reason is largely so that the administration can say it has a policy, but low priority is assigned to it and little is done to implement it. At the same time, it must be said that many academic scholars do not understand or sympathize with the fact that

policymakers must deal with difficult trade-off dilemmas between the quality of a policy and other desiderata. (On the
latter point, see chapter 2.)

* * * *

I have called attention to the somewhat different conceptions
of knowledge about international affairs that are valued most
in academia and in the world of policymaking. Also contributing to the gulf between these two cultures are the rather
different socialization experiences that shape an individual's
career orientation and professional style in the worlds of academia and policymaking. Those who participate in policymaking learn that little can usually be accomplished by individuals without a great deal of coordination, cooperation,
and compromise with others. And one gets ahead in government by being able to adapt to the norms and procedures of
various kinds of group work. The policymaking process
blends the search for a high-quality policy decision with the
need to develop a degree of consensus and support. Inter-
personal and negotiating skills as well as analytic competence
are at a premium. At the extreme, an individual occasionally
finds it preferable not to claim credit for a good idea but instead to plant it inconspicuously in the process of interacting
with others.

On the other hand, as is well known, efforts to cooperate
and coordinate often break down, and the policy process is
then driven by the dynamics of bureaucratic politics. When
the game of bureaucratic politics cannot be tamed by strong
leadership at higher levels, information and knowledge become instruments of the struggle between competing policy
advocates.

Academia is less conducive to participation in group work.
To get ahead one tries to differentiate one's ideas and scholarly products to give them a distinctive stamp. Importance is
attached to establishing an individual reputation rather than

a reputation for effective participation in group work. It is not surprising that academics who enter government often find that with the individualistic professional style into which they have been socialized they encounter difficulties in the world of policymaking. However, it must also be said that other academics entering the policy world adapt all too readily to tempting opportunities to participate in influencing policy. They become absorbed in the internal politics of policymaking and lose interest in strengthening the role of scholarly knowledge in policymaking. In my interviews I have found that such former academics are often more useful as informants on the process and politics of policymaking than on ways of strengthening and using substantive knowledge of policy problems.

## A Common Ground: Knowledge and Action

The most promising way to bridge the gap between the academician and the policymaker, I believe, is to focus on the relationship between knowledge and action in the conduct of foreign policy. That relationship, of course, must be conceptualized in a way that will speak to both academic scholars and policy specialists. What this means, more concretely, is that scholars should acquire a clear and detailed understanding of the types of knowledge policymakers need as they attempt to understand and to deal with different types of foreign policy problems. Scholars can be assisted to some extent in refining their understanding of the knowledge requirements of practitioners by what policy specialists themselves say they need. But since practitioners and their staff specialists may not be able to articulate knowledge requirements well enough, scholars will need to study actual policymaking closely to identify the types of theory and knowledge that are likely to be relevant.

Since so many individuals who serve as policy specialists

and in staff roles in the government have previously studied international relations in academic centers, they can and do serve as informal intellectual brokers between the two cultures. To the extent that they accept this role they are in a position to draw on and adapt the results of academic research for use in policymaking and, also, to familiarize academic specialists with the kinds of information and knowledge required by policymakers. How much interest they have in doing so and how well they perform this role, however, is another question. Nonetheless, it has been useful to interview a number of present and former policy specialists and intelligence officers with academic backgrounds in order to draw on their experience and to obtain their suggestions for better appreciating the relationship between knowledge and action.

\* \* \* \*

In concluding this chapter I return to one of Richard Goodwin's criticisms of Thomas Schelling's *Arms and Influence*. Goodwin argued that a "systematic theory" of the kind he (incorrectly) attributed to Schelling was impossible as well as dangerous. The criticism rests on a misunderstanding of systematic theory as something that seeks or seems to provide policymakers with detailed, high-confidence prescriptions for action in each contingency that may arise. I will argue that such a theory does not exist and is not feasible. The choice, however, is not between detailed, high-confidence prescriptions for action and nothing at all. I suggest that theory and generic knowledge may most feasibly and usefully contribute to the *diagnosis* of the specific situations with which policymakers must deal, rather than to *prescriptions* for action. My assumption is that correct diagnosis of a policy problem should precede and—as in much of medical practice—is usually a prerequisite for making the best choice from among policy options. The analogy with the medical profession is an apt one, since the policymaker, too, acts as a clinician in striving to make a correct diagnosis of a problem before determining how best to prescribe for it.

The reader will note that for Goodwin's rhetorical question whether a systematic theory is possible I have substituted three different questions: (1) What is the relationship between knowledge and action? (2) What kind of knowledge is most relevant for assisting policymaking? (3) How can *this* type of knowledge be developed by scholars and research specialists and how can it be employed effectively by policymakers?

# 2. The Role of Knowledge in Policymaking

Some persons interviewed for this study expressed a sober view of the prospects for improving foreign policy by developing and making available better knowledge of the various strategies and activities that enter into the conduct of foreign policy. Some who read an earlier draft of parts of this study thought I had underestimated the extent to which policy is determined by factors other than scholarly knowledge and competent policy analysis. A realistic view of how policy is actually made, they cautioned, would emphasize that political considerations in the shaping of policy often constrain the impact that objective analysis can have on the decisions taken. Others emphasized that top policymakers and policy professionals at lower levels are heavily influenced by their existing mind-sets in terms of how they view and deal with policy problems and in their receptivity to new ideas and analysis.

In fact, scholars who have studied policymaking are well aware of these characteristics of the policy process and the constraints they impose. However, many of them reject, as I do, the implication that even an improved body of policy-relevant knowledge would make little difference in improving the quality of many policy decisions and that, therefore, there is little point in urging the development of better scholarly knowledge of foreign policy problems and of better ways of using such knowledge in policymaking.

Of course, the policymaking system must be structured and managed to make it possible for policymakers to obtain relevant knowledge, when it exists, on a timely basis, and to encourage and facilitate use of it. I have found it useful in developing policy-relevant theory to distinguish between *substantive theory* and *process theory*. Substantive theory provides knowledge of standard foreign policy undertakings, instruments of policy, and strategies. Process theory focuses on how to structure and manage the policymaking process to increase the likelihood of producing more effective policies. Of course, substantive knowledge and process intersect as policy specialists analyze a problem and consider alternative options for dealing with it.[1] And of course various political and organizational factors and situational constraints come into play that may limit the impact of substantive knowledge.

When relevant general knowledge that bears on a particular type of policy problem is weak or nonexistent, these other factors are likely to have a stronger impact on policymaking. However, when policy-relevant knowledge is available, it can discipline and constrain the unfettered play of political factors in policymaking. This is not to say, however, that even robust policy-relevant knowledge can eliminate consideration of political factors by policymakers; rather, it provides the possibility of better disciplining and constraining such factors. The position I take here differs from that held by some students of policymaking who argue that the sole or dominant criterion of good policy should be its objective *analytical rationality*. Such a point of view reflects an overintellectualized view of foreign policy. In choosing from alternative options, policymakers typically must be concerned not merely with meeting the ideal of analytical rationality, but also with several other policy desiderata. To highlight the necessarily broader political concerns and interests that policymakers must take into account, I have coined the term *political rationality*.

It is admittedly difficult, then, to ensure that relevant substantive knowledge will have an optimal impact on policymaking. Assuming that it does enter the policymaking process, what kind of impact can it be expected to have? The position taken in this study is that policy-relevant knowledge can be expected to make a limited and indirect, but still quite useful, contribution. *General knowledge of international relations produced by scholars can be only an input to, not a substitute for, the policy analysis of a specific problem conducted within the government.* Policy analysts, not academic scholars, have the difficult task of adapting the available general knowledge of a given strategy or foreign policy undertaking to the particular case at hand. General knowledge can help with making the diagnosis of the situation that policymakers need, but the diagnosing also requires access to specific intelligence and information about the situation. Government policy analysts and policymakers have access to more of that information than scholars outside the government have.

Similarly, it should be emphasized, *general knowledge of a strategy or standard foreign policy undertaking is not a substitute for, but only an aid to, the final judgment of high-level policymakers.* (Incidentally, the same can be said regarding the results of intragovernmental policy analysis; it, too, is an aid to, not a substitute for, the judgment of policymakers.) This is so because these policymakers take into account various factors, such as domestic political considerations, international opinion, and value priorities, that cannot be anticipated by scholars who produce generalizations about foreign policy and cannot be taken into account or adequately weighed even by policy analysts. Thus, whereas scholars and policy analysts can and should preoccupy themselves with the task of identifying high-quality policy options (i.e., meeting the special criterion of analytical rationality) high-level policymakers must exercise broader judgments that take into account a variety

of additional considerations. What these additional considerations are will become clearer as we turn now to a discussion of what is meant by the "judgment" of policymakers to
which policy-relevant knowledge attempts to contribute.

## Judgment in Policymaking

The importance of judgment is often emphasized in discussions of policymaking. Individuals who have had experience
in policymaking regard judgment as a critical and indeed
necessary ingredient of policymaking, and for this reason,
they maintain, policymaking must be regarded as an art and
not a science. Yet the concept of judgment is seldom expli-
cated or studied and, therefore, despite its centrality in policymaking it remains ambiguous. Since judgment plays so important a role in bringing knowledge to bear on action, it is
necessary to try to identify more clearly what judgment consists of.

One way to proceed with this task is to replace the global
notion of judgment with an identification of those aspects of
decisional problems about which policymakers exercise judgment. At least seven different types of judgment need to be
distinguished from one another. A policymaker may feel obligated to make more than one type of judgment in arriving
at a particular decision, but it is unlikely that all or most of
the following types of judgment would enter into a particular
decision.

1. *Trade-off judgments.* One of the most important decisions
high-level policymakers are often obliged to make concerns
the trade-off between seeking to maximize the analytical
quality of the policy to be chosen and the need to obtain sufficient support for the policy option that is finally chosen. Another familiar, often difficult trade-off problem arises from
having to decide how much time and policymaking resources
to allocate to the effort to identify the best possible policy op-

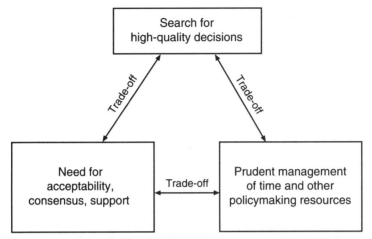

**Figure 2.1.** Trade-off dilemmas in policymaking. (Adapted from A. L. George, *Presidential Decisionmaking in Foreign Policy: The Effective Use of Information and Advice* [Boulder, CO: Westview Press, 1980], p. 2.)

tion. A third trade-off problem arises from having to decide how much political capital, influence resources, and time to expend in an effort to increase the level of support for the option to be chosen.

The three trade-off problems are depicted in figure 2.1.

Academic specialists can easily fall into the error of thinking about high-quality policy decisions in too narrow a framework. Policymakers have to deal with the tension that often exists between policy quality and the need to choose a policy that commands enough support. Very often a measure of quality has to be sacrificed in favor of a decision that will get the kind of political support within and outside the administration that is necessary if the policy is to have a chance of being sustained.

Another trade-off in political policymaking is the one between the quality of the decision and the policymaker's sensible use of time and of analytical and political resources. A policymaker who spends a tremendous amount of time trying to arrive at a policy decision of superior quality may incur considerable costs; time is not free. And if policymakers tie up all the analytical resources at their disposal in order to achieve a higher quality decision, the analysis of other policy issues may be neglected or shortchanged. (This trade-off is said to have been a problem with Kissinger's style when he dominated foreign policymaking in the Nixon administration.) Policymakers also face the practical question of deciding how much of the political capital and influence resources at their disposal they should expend in order to gain support for a higher quality decision.

Dealing with these trade-off problems requires policymakers to exercise ad hoc judgment, since well-defined rules are lacking. When such dilemmas arise, how, if at all, can policy-relevant theories and generic knowledge of international relations assist in exercising judgment? This question is all the more difficult to answer because theory and generic knowledge are most directly relevant in the search for policy options of high analytical quality. This is also the focus and objective of prescriptive models of "rational" policymaking, which pay little, if any, attention to the trade-off dilemmas identified here. In fact, I know of no theory or model of decision making that tells policymakers how best to manage trade-offs among quality, consensus, and management of time and policymaking resources.

Nonetheless, several ideas can be put forward regarding the relevance of theory and generic knowledge for dealing with some trade-off problems. Knowledge can be developed about strategies such as deterrence, coercive diplomacy, and crisis management, for example; distinctions can be made between strong and weak variants of these strategies and between conditions that favor success and conditions that are likely to hamper success. Knowledge of this kind should be helpful in deciding whether the trade-off of policy quality for enhanced support would be acceptable or whether it would jeopardize the success of the weaker variant of the strategy chosen in order to gain additional support. Of course, the need for support may sometimes push the policymaker in the other direction—toward adopting a stronger variant of a strategy when a milder one would be more appropriate.

There is another way theory and generic knowledge can contribute to a better understanding of the costs and risks of trade-offs between quality and consensus. As is well known, bargaining often takes place among advocates of different policy options, and at times the dynamics of bargaining weaken the role of objective analysis in the search for an option that different members of the policymaking group can agree on. Good analysis of a policy problem can equip policymakers to anticipate what kinds and degrees of effectiveness a high-quality option is likely to lose if trade-offs are made during the bargaining in order to gain broader support. In this view, *analysis is not a substitute for bargaining but serves to inform and discipline the bargaining process in a way that helps prevent ending up with a compromised policy that is likely to prove ineffectual.*

2. *Judgments of political side-effects and opportunity costs.* Still another type of trade-off dilemma must be recognized. The criterion of analytical rationality is applied most comfortably by the policymaker when the problem in question is "bounded"—that is, when it is insulated from other policy issues that are already on the agenda or may soon emerge. But many policy issues are imbedded in broader political and policy contexts. When this is so, the policymaker finds it necessary to consider what effect his choice on a particular policy issue will have on his overall political standing and on other parts of his overall policy program. In choosing what to do in situations of this kind the policymaker is guided not exclusively or even primarily by the dictates of analytical rationality but may be heavily influenced by his judgment of the political side-effects and opportunity costs of his choices. Of course,

this is not to say that a policy choice that is "best" when judged by the criterion of analytical rationality always conflicts with the decisionmaker's political interests—indeed it may enhance them—or that the analytically best policy choice on a particular issue will necessarily entail significant opportunity costs, but simply to recognize that such trade-off dilemmas often do arise.

3. *Judgments of utility and acceptable risk.* Policy analysts provide policymakers with relevant information for attempting to calculate the utility of different options. This task is often severely complicated by the inherent uncertainties regarding so many of the factors on which decisions and choices must be based. Although policy analysts attempt to identify relevant uncertainties and possible costs and risks, policymakers often perceive other possible costs and risks and other benefits that analysts have not considered. In the final analysis, it is the policymakers who must judge what costs and risks they are willing to accept in return for payoffs to which they attach particular value. Similarly, it is the policymakers who have to decide whether to choose an option that offers the possibility of a bigger payoff but is more risky or an option that offers less of a payoff but is less risky.

4. *Judgment about short-term and long-term payoffs.* Many policy problems pose a possible trade-off between short-term and long-term payoffs. The conventional wisdom of students of policymaking is that policymakers generally act to avoid short-term losses or to make short-term gains in preference to pursuing strategies for avoiding long-term setbacks or for long-range gains. Judgments of this kind are easier to make when policymakers are more certain of obtaining the short-term payoff than the long-term one. After all, the more distant future is laden with greater uncertainties than the near term. Moreover, short-term payoffs—either gains or avoided losses—tend to be more highly valued by most political leaders. However, not all trade-offs between short-term and long-term payoffs are so easily resolved, and these offer a greater

challenge for exercising judgment influenced by relevant knowledge and analysis of the problem.

5. *Satisfice or optimize?* Policymakers are often faced with the need to decide whether to settle for a limited payoff in a particular situation (i.e., to "satisfice") or to strive for a substantially greater one (i.e., to optimize). The literature on complex organizations emphasizes that they are generally programmed for satisficing. Political leaders, however, are able to display more variation in making such choices, and this is another type of judgment they are sometimes called on to make.

It would be interesting to study what role general knowledge and policy analysis play, or could play, in policymakers' judgment whether to satisfice or to optimize.

6. *Dealing with value complexity.* Many of the policy problems policymakers have to deal with are laden with competing values and interests. (These include, of course, not only the national interest of the country, insofar as it can be assessed, but also the personal and political stakes of the leader.) The standard textbook model of rational policymaking cannot be employed in such instances, because the multiple values embedded in the policy problem cannot be reduced to a single utility function that can then be used as a criterion for choosing among options.

In such cases, policymakers must exercise several kinds of judgment to deal with value complexity. Can a policy option be invented that may at least partially satisfy each of the competing values and interests? When such political creativity is not possible or is not forthcoming, policymakers have to judge value priorities. Which values and interests engaged by the policy problem are more important? What criterion of importance should be employed? If not all the values and interests embedded in the problem can be satisfied by the policy option that is selected, can additional policy measures be identified and put into effect later to offer some degree of satisfaction for the other values and interests? Once again, one can ask how general knowledge of international affairs and policy analysis can help policymakers deal with difficult issues raised by value complexity.

7. *When to decide?* Finally, policymakers are often called on to decide *when* a decision should be made. Policymakers may or may not delay making decisions to give analysts more time to come up with a better policy or to muster more support for their policy choice. But here we want to call attention to the fact that other considerations may influence policymakers' sense of the timing of a decision. The urgency of the policy problem itself, or domestic or international constraints or both, may influence the policymakers' judgment about when to decide on a policy, quite independently of the quality of analysis available.

\* \* \* \*

Perhaps this brief discussion of the various types of judgments policymakers must make from time to time suffices to provide a richer framework, albeit a more complicated one, for considering the extent to which general knowledge of international relations problems and policy analysis within the government can contribute to the decisions of policymakers. Quite obviously, scholarly knowledge and policy analysis can contribute more to some of the judgments policymakers make than to others. And, certainly, some types of judgments take precedence over—or are relatively insensitive to—the professional knowledge base that is analytically relevant for policymaking. In other words, there can be no assurance that even a well-developed knowledge base and competent policy analysis will have impact when policymakers are impelled to make judgments in reaction to other considerations.

The foregoing picture of how the policymaking process complicates and limits the likely impact of general knowledge of foreign policy activities and policy analysis on policy is indeed sobering. I will attempt to demonstrate that even "weak" theories and general knowledge of foreign policy problems *are* relevant nonetheless, and that their absence or the failure to make use of them in policymaking can mean the success or failure of policy.[2] Part two highlights this point by showing that lack of adequate conceptualization and general knowledge of several of the strategies employed by the United States toward Iraq in 1988–91 had something to do with the failure or mixed results of these policies.

Part Two

# The Inadequate Knowledge Base for
# U.S. Policy toward Iraq, 1988–91

# 3. Outcomes of U.S. Strategies toward Iraq

During the Iran-Iraq War the United States strongly tilted toward Iraq, furnishing it with substantial economic assistance and large amounts of indirect military aid to prevent Iran from achieving a hegemonic position in the Gulf and spreading its radical Islamic fundamentalism. This policy was based on familiar balance-of-power considerations, and it was successful. But at different stages in its relations with Iraq after the Iran-Iraq War, the United States employed a number of strategies that either failed to accomplish their purpose or produced mixed results. This chapter contains an overview of the development of U.S. policy toward Iraq between 1988 and 1991 and brief discussions of those strategies and their outcomes.

With the end of the Iran-Iraq War in August 1988, the question arose whether a change in U.S. policy was desirable or required. A few mid-level policy specialists in the Bush administration argued that balance-of-power considerations now dictated ending economic and military assistance to Iraq, since it had emerged from its successful war to constitute a potential new threat to regional stability.[1] These estimates were based not merely on balance-of-power logic but also on a belief that Saddam Hussein harbored ambitions for achieving hegemony in the region.

The argument for a change in U.S. policy toward Iraq, if indeed it reached the highest levels of the administration, received little consideration, for several reasons. First, an abrupt change or reversal of foreign policy is never easy in a democratic system; it must generally await a severe crisis that drives home unmistakably that the policy has become obsolete, that continuing it is dangerous, or that it no longer has domestic support. Even so, the change in policy may not occur until there is a change of administration. These prerequisites for a reversal of policy did not exist at the end of 1988. After all, the policy of massive assistance to Iraq to prevent its defeat by Iran had been successful. Although Washington's fear of an expansionist Iran had subsided for the time being, policymakers retained their image of a hostile, threatening regime in Tehran that would need to be "balanced" in the future. Contributing to this negative image of Iran was the legacy of the hostage crisis.

Granted that an abrupt reversal of policy would have been very difficult and that U.S. leaders could not be expected to quickly perceive new implications of balance-of-power logic, the question remains why, now that the war was over, the administration did not at least substantially reduce the flow of economic and indirect military assistance to Iraq. Evidently the Bush administration did not regard it as inevitable that Iraq, successful in its war with Iran, would pose a threat to the regional balance of power—the second reason why policy change was not seriously considered. The dominant mind-set of U.S. policymakers was that Iraq would continue to be preoccupied with attempting to recover from its destructive war with Iran and would not pose serious threats for some time. Washington did not perceive Saddam Hussein as committed to an expansionist foreign policy aiming at a hegemonic role, one that would constitute a new threat to U.S. and western interests in the region. And third, the administration no doubt wished to continue its policy of wooing Iraq away from the Soviet Union.

Although Saddam Hussein was generally regarded as a "bad actor," some encouragement was derived from the fact that he had moderated some aspects of his policies and behavior during the war with Iran. And it was hoped that Saddam might be disposed, if treated in a conciliatory and friendly way, to alter whatever hostility he may still have harbored to the conventional norms and practices of the international system and to evolve into a responsible, constructive actor in the Middle East. Some policy officials, but not all, thought Saddam could be "reformed" insofar as his external behavior might become more moderate and more acceptable, leaving aside the much less likely possibility of a moderation of his internally repressive regime.

Accordingly, to the extent that top officials in the administration gave serious thought to the matter, they did not judge it either necessary or advisable to curtail aid to Iraq and shift to a policy of containment and deterrence. Indeed, relations with Iraq were not a priority consideration for the president and his closest advisers during this period. Their attention was focused on the profound changes in the Soviet Union and Eastern Europe. As Don Oberdorfer notes, "Without attention at these high levels, the chances for a policy shift . . . are slim."[2]

In reflecting today on how they perceived the situation at that time, administration officials may well believe that to have shifted to a policy of containment and confrontation of Iraq was not a viable option; they may well believe that they really had no choice at the time but to continue the policy of constructive engagement and friendship toward Iraq. Even though policy officials may not have explicitly stated that the United States should help Saddam because he was redeemable, Washington's actions toward Iraq included elements not only of an effort to resocialize and reform a rogue leader but also elements of appeasement. (I use the term *appeasement* here in its original, nonpejorative sense. *Conciliation* and some connotations of *constructive engagement* are roughly equivalent in meaning to *appeasement*.) To the extent that policymakers even thought of undertaking a more confrontational policy toward Iraq, such a policy was regarded as not only unnecessary but also lacking domestic and international support, particularly among friendly Arab states in the region.

Be that as it may, the continuation of the policy of friendship appears to have been buttressed by two closely related tacit assumptions: first, that Iraq was still needed to balance the threat that Iran, though badly damaged by the war, would continue to pose to its neighbors and to U.S. interests in the region; and second, that by continuing to emphasize its desire for friendly relations with Saddam the U.S. could reform him.[3]

After the Gulf crisis erupted, administration leaders acknowledged that their policy had been to try to resocialize Saddam Hussein and that it had failed. President Bush was quoted as saying there had been "some reason to believe that perhaps improved relations with the West would modify his behavior." On another occasion after the bombing of Iraq started, the president stated to a reporter, "We tried the peaceful route; we tried working with him and changing [him] through contact. The lesson is clear in this case that it didn't work." More recently, in a press conference held on May 27, 1992, President Bush defended his pre–Gulf War policy toward Iraq, saying that his administration tried to work with Saddam "on grain credits and things of this nature to avoid aggressive action. And it failed. That approach, holding out a hand, trying to get him to renounce terrorism and join the family of nations, didn't work." And the president's special assistant for national security affairs, Brent Scowcroft, also acknowledged that the object of the earlier approach to Saddam was "to make this guy a reasonably responsible member of the international community."[4]

Members of the administration began to have some doubts

about the policy of friendship with Iraq in early 1990 when, in his speech of February 24, Saddam Hussein attributed hostile intentions to the United States and objected to its military presence in the Gulf and its role in the Middle East. A review of policy toward Iraq was undertaken in the spring by the Interagency Deputies Committee, headed by deputy national security adviser Robert Gates. That the policy was not working as it should and that it required some adjustments was recognized. A few inducements to Iraq for closer ties with the United States were removed, but it was agreed that the option of friendship with Iraq should be kept open, and most forms of assistance were continued.[5]

Participants in the policy review found it difficult to understand why Saddam had resorted to hostile rhetoric and accusations against the United States. At the same time, however, they could not see any reason for not continuing to hope that Saddam would moderate his behavior. It was decided to try to reassure the Iraqi leader that the United States wished to continue the policy of friendship, that it did not harbor hostile intentions toward Iraq, and that its military presence in the Gulf was not aimed at Iraq. At the same time, it was thought advisable to convey to Saddam diplomatically that the quality of the relationship between the two countries in the future would depend on Iraq's behavior. As assistant secretary of state John Kelly put it in his congressional testimony in late April, Iraq's difficult behavior was recognized and posed a challenge, but it remained important to provide Iraq with an opportunity "to reverse this deterioration of relations."[6] This message was conveyed in several ways—including a visit to Baghdad in May by Richard Haass, the National Security Council (NSC) specialist on Near East and South Asian affairs—but always in the context of Washington's desire to continue to seek friendship with Iraq.

When Saddam began openly menacing Kuwait in mid-July 1990 and then mobilized large forces on the border, the administration finally took a more sober view of his intentions.

A belated ad hoc effort was mounted to deter him in case he was planning to attack Kuwait. But the administration was able to put together only a weak deterrence strategy and, moreover, coupled its bland deterrence effort with official reassurances to Saddam that it continued to desire friendly relations—a dual strategy of deterrence and reassurance that failed to achieve its objective.

After Saddam's forces quickly overran Kuwait, the administration responded by mounting a strong deterrent effort to dissuade a further move against Saudi Arabia. Whether Saddam actually entertained such a plan and needed to be deterred remains uncertain, but he did not move against Saudi Arabia. From the administration's standpoint, the threat to Saudi Arabia lay not exclusively in the possibility of invasion. By taking over Kuwait and keeping sizeable Iraqi forces there, Saddam was in a position to intimidate Saudi leaders and influence them to go along with his wishes.

As for the objective of liberating Kuwait, the administration took the lead in obtaining UN Security Council approval for employing coercive diplomacy to persuade Saddam to remove his forces from Kuwait. Initially backed by a comprehensive set of economic sanctions, this variant of coercive diplomacy was later judged to be inadequate for achieving a timely and reliable success, and the idea of a "preventive war" to drastically weaken Iraq's military capabilities gained support. Without committing itself to this course of action, the administration decided to augment U.S. forces in the Gulf to create an "offensive capability," and it succeeded in persuading the Security Council in late November to adopt a new resolution embracing the strongest variant of coercive diplomacy, one that gave Saddam an ultimatum backed by the threat of overwhelming force.

To the surprise of many, though not all, officials, the ultimatum failed to induce Saddam to pull out of Kuwait. The war that followed was remarkably successful from the military standpoint, and policymakers were soon obliged to consider how the political objectives of the war could be furthered by military strategy and by the terms for ending the war. It was decided for various reasons to forgo a demand for Saddam's ouster (a move within the United Nations to declare him a war criminal subject to an international trial had been set aside earlier) and also to forgo military occupation of the country. The way Washington dealt with the termination of the war led quickly to disappointment and questioning of its strategy. (Note that U.S. News and World Report titled its book on the Gulf War *Triumph without Victory*.) It would be quite incorrect to go so far as to say that the U.S.-led coalition won the war but lost the peace. But important questions remain as to the nature of the peace, the fate of Saddam, and Iraq's future. Since the end of the war the United States and its coalition partners have returned to the strategy of coercive diplomacy based on a continuation of economic sanctions to ensure Iraq's compliance with UN terms and, at least in the case of the United States, to bring about Saddam Hussein's downfall.

Many months after the end of the war, the administration undertook a belated effort to organize a broad-based opposition to Saddam Hussein composed largely of Iraqi dissidents living outside the country. And in August 1992 the administration imposed a "no-fly zone" over southern Iraq, ostensibly to shield dissident Shi'ites from Iraqi air attacks but also to increase pressure for Saddam's ouster.

If he survives nonetheless, the remaining option will be containment and deterrence of a much weakened Iraq. More remote but not inconceivable is the possibility that eventually Saddam may be seen as a useful actor in the regional balance of power in case Iran emerges as a new threat.

✳ ✳ ✳ ✳

This brief review of U.S. policies toward Iraq in the past decade has highlighted the fact that several of the strategies employed to deal with that country and its leader at different junctures failed altogether. The list of strategic failures includes the early effort to reform and resocialize Saddam Hussein, which included an element of appeasement; the effort to deter him from attacking Kuwait; then the effort to use two strong variants of coercive diplomacy to persuade him to get out of Kuwait. Balancing the list of strategic failures to some extent are the strong deterrence effort that was mounted to dissuade Saddam from attacking or coercing Saudi Arabia and the mixed results, despite the overwhelming military victory, achieved by the strategy for war termination.

The question arises, therefore, how best to understand and explain these important strategic failures and to do so in a constructive way so that appropriate lessons may be drawn. Were these policy failures due, as I believe some of them were, to an imperfect understanding by policymakers of the nature and general requirements of the strategies that were employed? If so, then the lessons would point to the need to develop—or at least bring to the attention of policymakers in the future—better conceptual understandings of these strategies and better generic knowledge regarding the conditions on which their successful employment depends.

On the other hand, one needs to consider that perhaps some of these strategic failures were not conceptual, that policymakers did in fact have an adequate grasp of the nature and general requirements of these strategies. Then, the explanation for their failures may be found, as I believe to be the case, either in poor implementation of the strategies or in an inability to cope with severe situational constraints on more effective application of the strategies. Another possibility, of course, is that one or another of these strategic failures was due to a combination of conceptual inadequacies and poor implementation. Still another possibility that may apply to several of the strategic failures is that an incorrect image of Saddam Hussein held by U.S. policymakers contributed to their failure. Perhaps he was someone who could not be reformed, deterred, or (as some have argued) coerced.

I do not wish to leave the impression that the success or

failure of policy rested exclusively on whether the U.S. image of Saddam Hussein was correct or whether the quality of the conceptualization and general knowledge of the strategies that were employed was defective. Available information from open sources and interviews with several policy specialists also suggests a fundamental weakness, if indeed not a failure, of intelligence on critical matters throughout the period examined. In October of 1989, a year after the end of the Iran-Iraq War, the U.S. intelligence community assured the administration in a formal national intelligence estimate (NIE) that for the next two to three years Saddam Hussein would not pursue aggressive policies toward any of his neighbors but would focus on rebuilding his country and its economy.[7] Washington was well aware that Saddam Hussein's government was laboring under severe economic pressures as a result of its prolonged, costly war with Iraq. Intelligence was very slow, however, in asking why, then, Saddam was continuing to spend so much money on his ambitious military programs. It would have been possible to estimate that he was spending about a third of Iraq's gross national product on these military programs rather than giving greater priority, as the NIE assumed, to rebuilding his country and its internal economy, and to ask what this spending implied about his ambitions and plans. Coupled with this intelligence gap was a misplaced sense of assurance that we knew what we needed to know with regard to the approximate size and progress of Iraq's strategic weapons program and that we could reliably assess its current military capabilities. On the other hand, the five months that intervened between the onset of the crisis in early August 1990 and the onset of the air war in mid-January 1991 were effectively used by intelligence services to develop better information on targets in Iraq.

The weakness of the intelligence effort was perhaps magnified by the calculated, determined policy of friendship the administration was bent on pursuing toward Iraq. We know from studies of past cases that a firmly established policy provides a framework and atmosphere that can subtly discour-

age intelligence from contradicting existing policy and reduce policy specialists' receptivity to information that calls existing policy into question. The policy framework of pursuing
friendship with Saddam may well have reduced incentives to
ask more probing questions about Saddam Hussein's longer
range intentions. The commitment at the highest levels of
the administration to pursue friendship with Saddam Hussein may have discouraged intelligence and policy specialists
from a more vigorous challenge to the policy of continuing
to supply considerable economic and indirect military aid
to Iraq.

Later, after Iraqi forces occupied Kuwait and the United
Nations imposed economic sanctions, the intelligence community appears to have lacked the kind of knowledge of
Iraq's economy necessary for developing confident, reliable
assessments of the impact economic sanctions were likely to
have. The administration's lack of confidence in its ability to
predict the effect of sanctions and to assess the speed with
which Iraq's military would be able to produce weapons of
mass destruction played a role in its decision to shift to an
ultimatum backed by the threat of war.

In other respects, too, inadequate intelligence made policy
and its implementation more difficult. Limited knowledge of
Muslim culture, psychology, and ways of thought and expres-
sion added to the difficulty of inferring Saddam Hussein's
real beliefs, calculations, and intentions from his unusual
rhetorical style and added uncertainty to efforts to influence
him. Dealing with leaders from a culture so different from
our own added to the familiar problem of ensuring that what
one says is being understood and is taken seriously.

* * * *

It is not my purpose in the chapters that follow to provide a
detailed historical account of U.S. policy toward Iraq during
this period. Nor is it my purpose to contribute to political criticism of the administration's policy of friendship toward Iraq

or its other strategic failures. Rather, I wish to highlight the need to develop a better understanding of the nature of these strategies, the circumstances in which they are and are not likely to be viable policy choices, the requirements for their effective use and, more generally, the uses and limitations of each strategy as an instrument of foreign policy.

One can hope to make general observations along these lines that, though provisional, are plausible enough to stimulate additional analysis and reflection. Anticipating some of the conclusions to which the analysis will lead, I point out that some of these strategies have indeed not yet been adequately conceptualized either by scholars or by policy specialists. This point is true of the strategies of resocializing and reforming an outlaw state, appeasement, reassurance, and important aspects of war termination. In the chapters that follow I offer suggestions for better conceptualization of these four strategies. In addition, practical knowledge of all four of these strategies needs to be enhanced by more systematic, comparative analysis of historical experience—a type of knowledge that I refer to in this study as "generic knowledge," which comprises conditional generalizations. Scholars need to develop better conditional generalizations that will throw light on the uses and limitations of these strategies.

In contrast, both the conceptualization and the empirical knowledge of deterrence and coercive diplomacy were already well developed and, therefore, the failure of these strategies vis-à-vis Iraq is largely attributable to difficulties in applying them on this occasion. Careful analysis of the case should pinpoint these difficulties, thereby adding to a better understanding of implementation problems.

As noted in the Preface, the commentary on the various strategies that follows has benefited from discussions I have had with a number of policy specialists, several of whom read and commented on earlier drafts of part two. Some were participants in the policymaking process vis-à-vis Iraq, and others are policy analysts who take an interest in these matters.

# 4. Reforming Outlaw States and Rogue Leaders

The objective of resocializing and reforming a "rogue" leader, as the experience with Saddam Hussein indicates, is not easily achieved. The administration's effort to do so probably failed for a number of reasons. It appears to have been based on a defective conceptualization of the strategy, an incorrect image of Saddam Hussein, and a questionable and inconsistent application of the strategy of rewards and punishments. In addition, for reasons already noted in the discussion of the weakness of U.S. intelligence in chapter 3, Washington responded sluggishly to indications that the strategy was not working and that it had to be either revamped or replaced by containment and deterrence.

In part, too, though this was not the fundamental problem, Washington's sluggish response owed something to the fact that top-level policymakers were intensely preoccupied with developments in the Soviet Union and Europe and, as they admitted later, did not give enough attention to growing indications of Saddam's intentions.

The predominant mind-set of U.S. officials was that Iraq would continue to be preoccupied for some time with the onerous task of recovering from its destructive war with Iran.

Accordingly, Iraq was regarded as relatively unimportant in terms of policy priorities. I have been told that in much of 1990, before mid-July, the deterioration of relations with Iraq was not even the top priority of Near East policy specialists. Some were more concerned with the growing tension between India and Pakistan, which was complicated by the danger of additional nuclear proliferation. Other Middle East policy specialists were preoccupied with the Arab-Israeli conflict and were focusing on how to get a peace process started.

There is ample reason to believe that the administration's policy toward Saddam Hussein prior to the Gulf crisis was based squarely on the assumption that he could be encouraged to play a constructive, responsible role. This assumption was supported by evidence that Saddam had displayed restrained behavior during the Iran-Iraq War. This restraint seemed to indicate that he was moving toward greater moderation in attitudes and behavior.

This image of Saddam evidently played a fundamental role in the adoption of NSC Directive 26, October 1989, which set the basis for U.S. policy toward Iraq. As characterized by Don Oberdorfer, NSC Directive 26 had as its underlying premise that Baghdad had emerged from the war with Iran "prepared to play a more constructive international role."[1] Excerpts from the directive, declassified and made available to Congress in May 1992, stated that "normal relations between the U.S. and Iraq would serve our longer-term interests and promote stability in both the Gulf and the Middle East." The directive recognized important differences with Iraq over chemical and biological weapons, its nuclear aspirations, the state of human rights in Iraq, and its meddling in Lebanon and other Middle East states, but nonetheless held that "the U.S. Government should propose economic and political incentives for Iraq to moderate its behavior and to increase our influence with Iraq."[2] And, specifically, U.S. companies were to be encouraged to participate in the postwar reconstruction of Iraq as long as they did not abet nuclear proliferation.

Various indications in Saddam Hussein's behavior during the Iran-Iraq War encouraged U.S. policy to move in this direction:

- Iraq began to distance itself from the Soviet Union's policy in various Third World countries.
- Iraq became less hostile to the Arab-Israeli peace process.
- Saddam expelled some (though not all) leading terrorists.
- Iraq apologized and eventually paid $27 million in a compensation package for families of the thirty-seven victims of the Iraqi missile attack on the USS *Stark* in the Persian Gulf.
- Iraq agreed to restoring diplomatic relations with the United States and treated American officials in Iraq in a strikingly friendly way.
- Iraq eased restrictions on foreign travel.
- Access was given to Iraqi Kurdistan.[3]
- Iraq offered a substantial market for sale of U.S. agricultural products and investment opportunities.

Washington's perception that Iraq was moving in a moderate direction was reinforced by leaders of friendly Arab states who attached importance to the change in Saddam's behavior. The danger of mistaking a leader's tactically motivated good behavior as a sign of a more fundamental change is a familiar one in international relations.

Later, Saddam's speech of February 24, 1990, in which he attributed hostile intentions to the United States and objected to its naval presence in the Gulf was regarded by many members of the Bush administration as an emotional overreaction to a Voice of America (VOA) broadcast in Arabic that criticized secret police abuses in Iraq and other countries and seemed to call for overthrow of Saddam's regime.[4] This interpretation was held even by some area experts, whereas a few policy specialists took a more sober view of Saddam's speech, regarding it as a well-considered statement of his aspirations and his estimate of the strategic situation in the region. Lack of greater receptivity to this more sober interpretation of Saddam's statements and to later indications of his hegemonic ambitions is an example of the familiar psychological tendency to readily accept new information that supports existing beliefs and policies and to remain skeptical of developments that challenge the existing mind-set.[5] The administration's sluggish response until mid-July to growing indications that Iraq posed a possible threat and that it had been operating with a mistaken image of Saddam also exemplifies the well-known phenomenon of an established policy that acquires a momentum of its own and is difficult to reverse until it fails unmistakably (see chapter 3).

The importance of President Bush's continued commitment to the policy of friendship with Iraq should not be overlooked. The basic assumptions of a policy are not easily challenged by others within the policymaking system when a high-level policy has strong presidential commitment.

* * * *

The Great Powers are often confronted by ambitious states that are not socialized into the norms of the international system and pose a threat to its orderly workings and stability. Addressing this problem at the outset of his book *A World Restored*, Henry Kissinger held it to be of critical importance for the stability of the international system that all major states and their leaders hold a common concept of "legitimacy," which he defined as "international agreement about the nature of workable arrangements and about the permissible aims and methods of foreign policy." Kissinger referred to states that rejected the norms and practices of the existing international system as "revolutionary" states.[6] (An important distinction needs to be made between "revolutionary" or "outlaw" states and "revisionist" states, which seek merely to rectify the status quo and do not reject the norms and practices of the international system.)

Outlaw states and their rogue leaders refuse to accept and abide by some of the most important norms and practices of the international system. Such states may seek to dominate and reshape the system to their own liking, and they may aim at global or regional hegemony. Some of them resort to practices such as state terrorism and taking as hostages citizens or official representatives of other states.

The Great Powers traditionally have accepted some responsibility for maintaining an orderly international system. Their incentive to find ways of coping with the threat to order by revolutionary powers, outlaw states, and rogue leaders is understandably accentuated when their own important national interests are threatened by the aims and behavior of such actors. It should be noted, however, that there exists no clear and commonly accepted definition of an outlaw or rogue state. These concepts have no standing in international law, and the United Nations works imperfectly to single out such offenders and deal with them. In fact, members of the international community may disagree among themselves whether the behavior of a certain state justifies its being regarded as an outlaw and treated as a pariah. Even behavior that violates a particular norm may be condoned by some as an understandable way of pursuing legitimate grievances or ambitions. Much of the task of recognizing and coping with outlaws, then, is undertaken by individual states, usually one or more of the Great Powers, which have a stake in preserving the system that they have helped to create and that they subscribe to, as well as in protecting interests threatened or damaged by an outlaw. At the same time, it should be recognized that efforts by one or more states to cope with outlaws do not always win agreement and support from other states; resocialization of the rogue leader then becomes all the more difficult.

What strategies, then, are available for dealing with revolutionary and outlaw states and their rogue leaders? Which strategies have been tried in the past and with what results? I have been unable to find any systematic, comparative study of these questions that would provide today's policymakers with theory and empirical knowledge of this phenomenon.[7]

It is not difficult to make a list of possible strategies. Some of the possibilities are the following:

- Military action, coercive pressures, or covert action, or all three, to replace the outlaw regime with a more acceptable government or to eliminate its rogue leader.[8]
- Containment, which, if pursued effectively and long enough, might help to bring about (as it did in the case of the Soviet Union) changes in ideology and the internal composition of the regime that lead to moderation in its foreign policy orientation and behavior.
- A strategy of rewards and punishments designed to bring about fundamental changes in behavior and attitudes, that is, an adaptation of the psychological technique of behavior modification for use in diplomacy. (Use of a behavior modification strategy probably must be accompanied by containment that prevents the outlaw state from achieving flagrantly expansionist aims.)

It should be noted that I have not listed appeasement as a strategy for dealing with outlaw states. When an outlaw state not only rejects important norms of the international system but also seeks major changes in the status quo, appeasement of even its legitimate and seemingly reasonable demands is unlikely to contribute to resocializing it into accepting the norms of the international system. In fact, such a strategy is much more likely to reinforce the rogue leader's ambitions and strengthen his predisposition to challenge the system (see chapter 5). Nevertheless, limited appeasement may have to be resorted to occasionally as a time-buying strategy for determining the true character of the adversary, strengthening one's capabilities, or generating domestic and international support for resisting the outlaw more effectively later.

In this connection, the strategy of *conditional reciprocity*—

demanding meaningful changes in policy and behavior in return for each concession or benefit—is safer and likely to be
more effective than pure appeasement in achieving resocialization in the long run. In scholarly writings conditional reciprocity is usually treated as a tactic to be employed in negotiating a particular issue or in encouraging changes in one or
more of an adversary's policies. Here, however, we point to its
strategic use as part of a long-range effort for bringing about
fundamental change in the nature of the outlaw state and its
leadership, that is, the gradual replacement of its antipathy
to the norms and practices of the international system with
attitudes and behavior more supportive of that system. In
other words, conditional reciprocity may be used as a lever
for implementing the strategy of behavior modification, to
which we will turn shortly, and the objective of resocializing
the outlaw state and reforming its rogue leadership. At the
same time, one should keep in mind that conditional reciprocity can also be used for the lesser objective of inducing a
change in the policies of another actor, whether that actor is
an outlaw state or a responsible adherent of the norms and
practices of the international system.

In any case, the strategy of resocialization and the levers it
employs must be conceptualized in a sophisticated way and
carefully implemented. This is easier said than done, in part
because we have as yet virtually no systematic analyses of past
efforts of this kind.

Nonetheless, it is possible to differentiate the use of rewards and punishments in a strategy of resocialization from
the use of rewards and punishments in two other strategies,
GRIT (graduated reciprocation in tension reduction) and "tit
for tat," which have different and more limited aims than the
resocialization strategy. GRIT is not a strategy for resocializing and reforming outlaw states. Rather, it has the much
more limited aim of removing distrust between states and
thereby paving the way for a relaxation of tensions. GRIT
attempts to do so by taking a series of meaningful conciliatory

actions, which may include concessions, carefully chosen to impress on the adversary that one genuinely desires to bring about an improvement in the relationship. These conciliatory actions are intended to encourage the adversary to replace his distrust with a more trusting, open attitude that will result in a relaxation of tensions, thereby creating an opportunity for dealing with some of the underlying disagreements that divide the two sides. Unlike conditional reciprocity, GRIT means initiating conciliatory actions without demanding that the adversary respond to the first conciliatory action with one of his own. And in contrast to the strategy of behavior modification, which rewards the subject only after he makes the desired change in behavior, GRIT offers its conciliatory actions beforehand, to induce a change in the adversary's perceptions and attitudes.

Given the striking differences between GRIT on the one hand and conditional reciprocity and behavior modification on the other, policymakers have a clear choice between options that differ both in the objective sought and in the way in which they offer positive inducements for that purpose. The risks of GRIT, should it fail, are limited by choosing conciliatory actions that, though meaningful in the eyes of the adversary, do not give away anything of major importance. Further implementation of GRIT is abandoned if after several conciliatory gestures the adversary gives no sign of adopting a more trustful attitude and desiring to cooperate in a relaxation of tensions.[9]

In principle, therefore, GRIT is not to be confused with the practice of offering bribes to secure the more ambitious aim of a change in the adversary's policies and behavior. Offering a reward in advance of a change in behavior (i.e., a bribe) is not consistent with the principle of behavior modification. Conditional reciprocity, on the other hand, can be a bit more flexible than behavior modification: it can encompass initiating a positive action in order to elicit an appropriate reciprocating move from the adversary. But if the adversary does not reciprocate, it is highly questionable whether additional positive moves would be consistent with the strategy of conditional reciprocity.

This somewhat abstract conceptual discussion of alternative strategies is useful only up to a point in policymaking. There are uncertainties in gauging whether the adversary is likely to be more receptive to one approach than to another or, indeed, to any of them. Policymakers may have to operate without reliable knowledge of the opponent's receptivity and likely response. And it may be difficult to correctly interpret the adversary's response. Intelligence sources and diplomatic communication may be helpful in reducing these uncertainties but are not likely always to eliminate them.

Thus, willingness to experiment and rely on trial and error may be necessary. However, the differences among the strategies should not be ignored or blurred in practice. For example, it is possible that at various times the Bush administration's policy of friendship toward Saddam Hussein blurred the important differences among GRIT, bribes, conditional reciprocity, and behavior modification. To the extent that blurring occurred, it would have further complicated the already difficult task of evaluating the efficacy of the policy of friendship and taking appropriate corrective measures.

As for the time-honored, if not always effective, practice of tit for tat, it received fresh attention during the Cold War as a possible strategy for eliciting cooperative behavior between actors whose mutual interests call for cooperating to avoid the worst possible outcome for both but who cannot easily do so because they are caught in a "prisoners' dilemma" (PD) situation. The relationship between a Great Power and the outlaw state it is attempting to reform, however, is not at all similar to the relationship between actors caught in a PD. The PD game is built on the premise that in a given situation the two sides have a latent interest in cooperating to avoid the worst possible outcome of their interaction; the challenge of the game for them is to act toward each other in ways that secure the better outcome that both prefer. The results of a computer simulation devised by Robert Axelrod indicated that in repeated plays of the PD game the tit-for-tat strategy performed best in achieving cooperation. This strategy bears a resemblance to some forms of conditional reciprocity in calling for each side to reward a conciliatory move by the other with a conciliatory move of its own and for responding to a hostile move with a negative one of its own until the two sides eventually converge in trading only positive moves; hence "cooperation" is established.[10] However, unlike tit for tat, which is a symmetrical game, resocialization is an asymmetrical game; one actor attempts to bring about fundamental changes in the attitudes as well as the behavior of the other. The use of rewards and punishments in resocialization strategy has to be much more refined and more finely calibrated.

Efforts to use conditional reciprocity on behalf of the resocialization objective are more likely to make headway when leaders of the outlaw state have begun to question the results of their antipathy to certain norms and practices of the international system and, having become somewhat disenchanted with their earlier policies, are now willing to question the assumptions on which those policies were based.

Consideration should be given to building into the practice of conditional reciprocity "tests" designed to find out whether the leaders of the outlaw state are genuinely moving toward abandoning earlier hostile attitudes and are ready to accept the norms and constraints of the international system. If they are not, the conclusion may be justified that the opposing leaders cannot be resocialized and that the only alternative is containment or efforts to bring about their replacement by more tractable leaders.

In employing conditional reciprocity as a lever, what one "gives" the outlaw state and what one demands in return require strategic planning. A series of incremental steps must be planned or improvised, yet the strategy must be implemented flexibly on the basis of monitoring and feedback. There must be awareness of the risks of the strategy and ways of minimizing and controlling those risks, and sensitivity to indications that the strategy is not working and needs prompt reassessment.[11]

In all these respects it appears that the administration's efforts vis-à-vis Saddam fell short of what was needed and contributed to failure.

What, then, are some of the risks of the strategy of conditional reciprocity and ways of minimizing them? It is not yet possible to derive firm answers to this question from studies of historical cases in which something like the strategy of conditional reciprocity was employed. In the meanwhile, by drawing on general principles of behavior modification and learning theory, some hypotheses can be formulated as to the risks of the strategy and possible ways of minimizing or avoiding them.[12] In listing these hypotheses here, I also raise the question whether these risks were adequately understood in the administration's policy toward Saddam Hussein.

1. Concessions and benefits bestowed should not be linked merely with general injunctions to improve behavior, and they should not be provided simply on the basis of the outlaw's vague assurances of better behavior. Rather, the offer of benefits should be coupled with a demand (however diplomatically conveyed) for quite specific changes in behavior that the outlaw state understands and agrees to. This approach is consistent with a cardinal principle of the psychological technique of behavior modification, which emphasizes that the therapist must identify for the subject the specific behavior that is to be extinguished and the more appropriate, acceptable specific behavior that should replace it. (Of course, it is possible that the outlaw state will refuse to accept the linkage of benefits to be received with some or all of the behavior changes demanded.)

2. Benefits generally should not be bestowed on an outlaw state in advance for reciprocity at some later date. Doing so

violates another basic principle of behavior modification, which emphasizes positive reinforcement by means of a reward *after* the subject has performed required behavior and rejects the alternative practice of offering a bribe in advance to elicit the required behavior.[13]

3. The concessions and benefits bestowed on an outlaw state should be capable of being withdrawn or at least terminated if its leaders renege on their part of the reciprocal arrangement. If the concessions are not reversible, they should be in the nature of acceptable losses and the outlaw state should be punished in some other way for its delinquency.

4. Insofar as possible, concessions and benefits should give leaders of the outlaw state and its people a stake in continuing the process of conditional reciprocity and an awareness of the advantages of accepting and participating in the international system. (This is probably what Henry Kissinger had in mind when, during the détente of the early 1970s, he spoke of weaving a "web of incentives" to encourage Soviet leaders to enter into playing a more "constructive" role in international affairs).

I have provided a provisional sketch of conditional reciprocity, its general requirements, and some of its risks. It should be obvious that this strategy is not assured of success and that its chances of succeeding may depend on a slow, incremental, patient application of conditional reciprocity. In addition we must recognize the following three complicating factors that may jeopardize efforts to pursue this strategy, all of which probably played a role in U.S. policy toward Iraq during and after the Iran-Iraq War.

1. The Great Power antagonist may need the outlaw state's support to orchestrate an effective balance of power against an aggressive third party.

2. The Great Power may mistake tactically motivated good behavior by the outlaw state as evidence of a strategic change for the better in that state's orientation to the norms of the international system.

3. Even a coherent, well-conceptualized long-range policy for attempting to resocialize the outlaw state may not be implemented consistently for various reasons. For example, the Great Power may be distracted by other foreign policy problems; obtaining and maintaining domestic and international understanding and support for the long-range resocialization policy may be difficult; bureaucratic officials may fail to implement policy fully or to correctly understand the policy laid down by top policymakers; and intra-administration disagreements on specific policies toward the outlaw state may undermine a more purposeful and consistent use of rewards and punishments. (These difficulties of implementation, of course, are not unique to the task of carrying out a policy of resocialization; they are also encountered in the conduct of foreign policy more generally.)

I noted earlier the absence of any systematic scholarly study of past efforts to reform outlaw states and to draw their leaders into acceptance of the norms and practices of the international system. The several hypotheses provided in this chapter about the requirements and modalities of resocialization need to be assessed through comparative studies of past efforts of this kind, some successful and others not. The absorption of Kemal Ataturk's Turkey into the international system is an example of successful integration of what was regarded initially, particularly by the British, as a possible outlaw state or, at least, as one situated outside the international community. In the contemporary era, efforts to deal with Iran, Vietnam, and Cambodia will be worth studying from this standpoint.

The Nixon-Kissinger détente policy probably constitutes an example of a flawed version of the strategy of resocialization insofar as its objectives included the long-range one of encouraging the Soviets to mend their ways and enter into a new "constructive relationship" with the United States. The development of a more constructive relationship between the two superpowers was to serve as the foundation for a new international system—what Nixon vaguely referred to as "a stable structure of peace." However, as many commentators noted, Nixon and Kissinger do not appear to have clearly conceptualized or elaborated what they had in mind in this respect. To be sure, the grand strategy for achieving this long-range objective combined rewarding the Soviets for good behavior with punishing them for unacceptable behavior. In other words, it was a carrot-and-stick strategy that attempted to employ, although imperfectly, behavior modification and conditional reciprocity. The conciliatory component of the strategy offered the Soviet Union a number of benefits it prized: the possibility of greater trade and more access to western credits, grain, and technology; the possibility of enhanced international status and recognition as a superpower equal to the United States; and the possibility of agreeing to the Soviets' long-standing desire for formal recognition of the territorial changes in Eastern Europe and acceptance of the Soviet Union's dominant position in that area.

In return, Nixon and Kissinger hoped that once the Soviet Union acquired a strong stake in the détente process it would act with restraint in the Third World lest it jeopardize benefits it was receiving from the evolving relationship. In the meantime, when the Soviets misbehaved in the Third World, Nixon attempted to react sharply. In this context U.S. leaders urged on the Soviets in general terms the necessity to adhere to a new set of norms and rules of conduct for restraining competition and avoiding conflict throughout the world. The underlying premise was that if these efforts were effective, not only would such norms and rules evolve over time but they would eventually be internalized by Soviet leaders and shape their behavior thereafter.

The strategy of resocialization in this case was flawed both conceptually and in implementation. Aside from attempting to weave a web of incentives to induce restraint in Soviet foreign policy—or, as one commentator put it, to create a new type of Soviet self-containment—it was not clear what reshaping of the international system Nixon and Kissinger had in mind. Lack of specificity in this respect perhaps contributed to Soviet failure to go along. Also, use of the reward-and-punishment strategy did not conform optimally with the conditional reciprocity and behavior modification strategies.

The détente policy foundered for other reasons as well. The two sides did not hold the same understanding of détente, and they held divergent expectations of its benefits. And the administration was not successful in achieving and maintaining domestic understanding and support for what it was trying to accomplish.[14]

The more recent substantial change in Soviet foreign policy and in its orientation to the international system associated with Gorbachev's "New Thinking" evolved more in line with George Kennan's 1947 "Mr. X" analysis, which held that effective containment for a period of years could eventually bring about internal changes in the ideology and domestic system of the Soviet Union that would result in a mellowing of its foreign policy.

As an example of a failed attempt to reform a rogue leader, one should look closely at Neville Chamberlain's policy toward Hitler. Sometimes forgotten or overlooked is the fact that Chamberlain did not only aim at appeasing Germany's legitimate revisionist claims but also hoped to bring Germany as a responsible actor into a reconstituted European system. As already noted, the Bush administration's policy toward Saddam Hussein prior to his invasion of Kuwait reflects another unsuccessful, and in many respects poorly conceived and implemented, effort to resocialize and reform him.

Other states and rulers that have been and still seem seriously at odds with the existing international system include the Iran of Ayatollah Khomeini's successors, Khaddafi's Libya, Assad's Syria, and Kim Il Sung's North Korea. It would be desirable to include in a comparative study an analysis of the policies the United States has employed to deal not only with the threats it perceives these states and their rulers pose for its own interests but also with their challenge to the norms and practices of the international system.

More systematic knowledge regarding the uses, limitations, and risks of the strategy of attempting to reform an outlaw state is not merely of historical or theoretical interest. Rather, it has considerable relevance for contemporary U.S. foreign policy. For example, in early 1992 the administration formally reviewed U.S. policy toward Iran in order to consider adopting a strategy of constructive engagement that would entail lifting some economic sanctions. According to the *New York Times*, the policy review, completed in April, concluded that any gesture that "might be politically meaningful in Tehran—lifting the ban on oil sales to America, for example—would have been politically impossible at home. On the other hand, a reward small enough to be painless in American political terms, such as lifting the ban on exports of carpets and pistachios, would have seemed too petty to Tehran." The policy review's conclusion that the time was not propitious for adopting a new policy is said to have been influenced by the earlier failure of constructive engagement toward Iraq. According to the *New York Times*, "even those analysts who defend the use of incentives to moderate behavior are bewildered about how to treat Iran," recognizing that the Iranian government's moves to curb radical elements and to expand ties with the West may be only a tactical maneuver that could be reversed when Iran succeeded in reconstructing its economy.[15]

# 5. Appeasement as a Strategy for Conflict Avoidance

> To show stubborn unyieldness to an opponent who possesses a real sense of grievance over specific issues may be as dangerous as to make concessions to an opponent whose ambitions are endless.—Evan Luard[1]

Elements of appeasement can be seen in the policy of friendship the United States pursued toward Iraq until the Persian Gulf crisis erupted in late July 1990. Whether one wishes to call it appeasement or prefers the term *conciliation* or *constructive engagement*, a review of that policy warrants the observation that it was neither well conceptualized nor well implemented. In any case, it will be useful to discuss here the nature of appeasement and its uses and limitations.

Many students of international relations have noted that the failure of the western powers to thwart the early aggressive moves of Japan and Hitler's Germany in the 1930s had a profound impact on subsequent American foreign policy attitudes. The lesson of Chamberlain's abortive effort to appease Hitler at Munich in 1938 has been deeply etched in the consciousness of successive generations of policymakers and foreign policy specialists. There is ample evidence that on numerous occasions since the end of World War II American policymakers have been influenced by the simple proposition "If appeasement, then World War III."

"Appeasement" became such an invidious phenomenon that little effort was made by policymakers and scholars alike to differentiate between those special conditions under which appeasement was indeed a misguided and dangerous policy and other conditions when it could eliminate the sources of conflict and the possibility of war with another state. Seventeen years after Fred Iklé deplored the undiscriminating condemnation of appeasement, the distinguished Australian international relations scholar J. L. Richardson could still observe that the contribution of contemporary theories of international relations to the study of appeasement "has been disappointingly limited."[2] At the same time, however, Richardson's own contribution focused almost exclusively on Chamberlain's abortive effort to appease Hitler.

A serious scholarly effort is only now under way to make a systematic comparative analysis of a variety of historical cases. The purpose of that analysis is to identify the conditions under which appeasement is a viable conflict avoidance strategy and other conditions in which appeasement is misguided and may well contribute to the eventual onset of war.[3]

The classic definition of appeasement is a simple one. In the language of diplomacy employed in the European balance-of-power system, *appeasement* referred to a policy of attempting to reduce tension between two states by the methodical removal of the principal causes of conflict between them. In this sense appeasement was regarded as a strategy for eliminating the potential for war in a conflict-ridden relationship between two states.[4] Whereas the classic definition refers to the removal of all the principal causes of conflict in the relationship, partial appeasement is also possible, leaving some sources of conflict untouched. The definition of appeasement leaves unanswered the important question of how to go about removing causes of conflict in a relationship with another state and makes no reference to the risks of embarking on this strategy or to ways of reducing or at least controlling such risks.

Appeasement has a much more ambitious conflict-avoidance goal than some other ways of moderating a conflictful relationship. In the classic European balance-of-power system the gradation among different steps for improving relations between two states was incorporated into well-defined and well-understood concepts and practices of diplomacy. These practices and the possible sequence in a gradual step-by-step improvement of relations are depicted in figure 5.1.

The process of improving relations might begin with *détente,* the mere relaxation of tensions, and possibly develop into *rapprochement,* whereby one or both sides express a desire to address some or all of their disagreements with a view to possible agreement. Rapprochement could lead to *entente*—a limited but significant improvement in relations in which the two sides recognize at least a similarity of views and interests but in which understandings are limited to certain issues and the improvement in the relationship stops short of an alliance. Entente could lead to either *appeasement* or *alliance* or both.

After the breakup of the European balance-of-power system, sharp distinctions among these terms were badly eroded. For example, the term *détente,* which came back into fashion after the Kennedy-Khrushchev effort to improve U.S-Soviet relations after the Cuban missile crisis, has acquired elasticity and ambiguity; the old meaning of a mere relaxation of tensions is often confused now with what used to be called "rapprochement," "entente," and even "appeasement." Elements of all three were implicit in Nixon's so-called détente policy. One reason why Nixon and Kissinger stretched the word *détente* to tacitly include these other objectives was that in the atmosphere of the Cold War it would

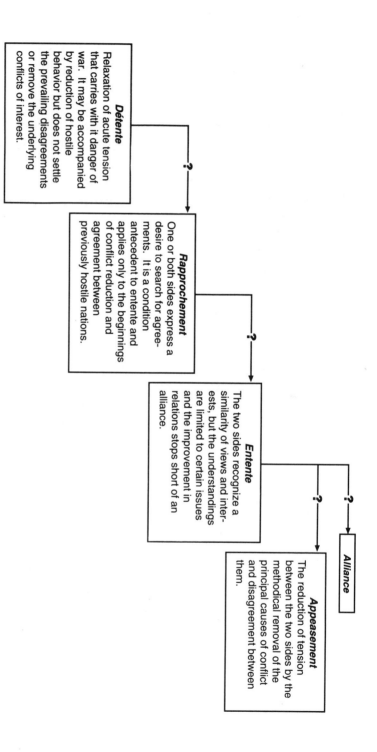

**Détente**

Relaxation of acute tension that carries with it danger of war. It may be accompanied by reduction of hostile behavior but does not settle the prevailing disagreements or remove the underlying conflicts of interest.

**?**

**Rapprochement**

One or both sides express a desire to search for agreements. It is a condition antecedent to entente and applies only to the beginnings of conflict reduction and agreement between previously hostile nations.

**?**

**Entente**

The two sides recognize a similarity of views and interests, but the understandings are limited to certain issues and the improvement in relations stops short of an alliance.

**?**

**Appeasement**

The reduction of tension between the two sides by the methodical removal of the principal causes of conflict and disagreement between them.

**?**

**Alliance**

**Figure 5.1.** Steps in improving relations between two states. The question marks indicate that the process need not go beyond détente and could stop at any point. (Reproduced from G. A. Craig and A. L. George, *Force and Statecraft: Diplomatic Problems of Our Time*, 2d ed. [New York: Oxford University Press, 1990], p. 250.)

have been most imprudent to refer to the more far-reaching objectives of their policy toward the Soviet Union explicitly in these terms.[5]

In contemporary writings on conflict resolution the term *conciliation* is often employed for *appeasement*. The latter term has acquired such a bad odor that specialists who write on these matters seem to gingerly steer clear of it. Let us turn now to discussing some of the conditions under which appeasement might be considered by policymakers, the strategies and tactics by means of which it might be pursued, its risks, and some possible ways of avoiding and controlling them. The discussion will focus on the possible attractions of the strategy of appeasement for strong states that enjoy a position of relative security, such as England in the nineteenth century and the United States in the post–World War II era. Appeasement is a much more difficult, problematic strategy for weak states, such as Israel, which exist in a precarious security environment; for them, reliance on deterrence generally appears preferable to appeasement, particularly when the relationship with adversaries approximates a zero-sum conflict.

Policymakers may consider a strategy of appeasement or conciliation when confronted by (1) a *revisionist* opponent who advances what it believes are legitimate claims for a change in a status quo situation, (2) an aggressive *expansionist* adversary, or (3) an opponent who is both revisionist and expansionist. (The discussion of appeasement focuses exclusively on whether to employ the strategy toward an adversary, not toward an ally or friendly state that pursues revisionist or limited expansionist aims.)

Policymakers must have a correct image of the opponent and his intentions and aspirations to differentiate among these three situations, but ascertaining the true character of the opponent may be difficult for some time. In addition to trying to determine whether the adversary is revisionist or expansionist or both, it is important to decide whether one is dealing with an outlaw state whose leaders essentially reject the norms and practices of the international system and are disposed to behave in ways that will undermine the order and stability of the system. Appeasement of such actors is neither desirable nor feasible, given their destructive orientation to the existing international system (see chapter 4).

On the other hand, when the adversary is not an outlaw but advances either revisionist or expansionist claims, the basic policy choices are conciliation, deterrence, or some combination of the two. Appeasement need not and often should not attempt to satisfy all of the revisionist or expansionist aims of the other party in a single grand settlement. There may be advantage in conducting appeasement in a careful, incremental fashion. Appeasement can thereby be incorporated into a strategy of conditional reciprocity by means of which one secures compensating concessions or assurances of one kind or another from the adversary.

Appeasement can aim at either a limited reduction or a comprehensive elimination of the conflict potential in the relationship with the adversary. Partial appeasement—that is, appeasing some of the adversary's demands—may be regarded as an acceptable short-term strategy for defusing a war-threatening crisis. But even if partial appeasement is successful in this respect, other sources of conflict in the relationship remain that may provoke new crises and military conflict in the future. Or appeasement can have the more ambitious objective of thoroughly removing, either in one move or incrementally, all major sources of conflict in the relationship.

Another useful distinction is between *passive appeasement* and *active appeasement*. Passive appeasement is the practice of not explicitly agreeing to, but not opposing, the adversary's alteration of a status quo situation—for example, France's acceptance of Hitler's occupation of the Rhineland. Active appeasement, on the other hand, is a diplomatic agreement that acquiesces to a forthcoming alteration of the situation—for example, the Munich agreement with Hitler, which accepted the forthcoming incorporation of the Sudetenland portion of Czechoslovakia.

In the absence of systematic research on past efforts to employ appeasement, there is no basis for articulating an operational theory or generic knowledge of this strategy that might help policymakers decide whether appeasement and conciliation would be a viable strategy. But practitioners should consider a number of questions when deciding between conciliation and deterrence in the face of demands for a change in the status quo.

1. Are the adversary's objectives revisionist or expansionist? If expansionist, are they of a limited, acceptable character?

2. Will appeasement of the adversary whet his appetite and encourage him to pursue new expansionist aims? Will the adversary view concessions as evidence of goodwill, friendship, and recognition of the legitimacy of his revisionist claims, or as evidence of irresolution and weakness and therefore a temptation to seek greater gains?

3. Can the adversary be appeased in such a way as to avoid giving the impression at home and abroad that one has yielded to blackmail? Will appeasement of the adversary result in serious damage to one's reputation in the eyes of other states and encourage them to advance revisionist or expansionist demands of their own?

4. How can one limit or control the various risks of appeasing another state? By drawing a line as to the extent of concessions that will be made? By appeasing individual claims incrementally? By obtaining credible formal assurances from the adversary that his demands for changes in the status quo are limited? Can tests be devised to assess the scope of the adversary's intentions?

5. Is the expected benefit of appeasing the adversary limited to the short-term objective of avoiding a crisis or war? Or

can short-term appeasement on a specific issue be built into a longer range strategy of turning the entire conflictful relationship into a cooperative one?

6. Is reliance on deterrence instead of appeasement a better strategy for coping with the adversary's hopes and demands for a change in the status quo? Will successful deterrence induce the adversary to give up hopes and efforts for changing the status quo in the future? Or will it only strengthen his motivation and lead him to prepare for challenging deterrence more effectively in the future? Beyond its psychological impact, will the change in the status quo in the adversary's favor that is being considered significantly alter the relative power balance?

The last of these questions highlights the need for studying a variety of historical cases to better understand the conditions under which appeasement or deterrence is likely to be a more effective conflict avoidance strategy. In an adaptation of one of Stephen Rock's suggestions, four possible situations and scenarios can be identified for analytical purposes, though policymakers can expect difficulty judging, especially at first, which of these four possibilities correctly identifies the case at hand:[6]

1. Either appeasement or deterrence can succeed, at least in the short run. A possible example is the Falkland Islands crisis, in which the British might have avoided the invasion of Argentina and the ensuing war through either a more robust deterrence effort or timely appeasement.

2. Neither deterrence nor appeasement is likely to succeed, because the adversary is bent on employing military force. A possible example is Hitler's determination to go to war against Poland in the autumn of 1939.

3. Only deterrence can succeed, because the adversary would respond to appeasement by generating new demands.

A possible example is Chamberlain's appeasement of Hitler on the Sudetenland question, which did not prevent him from occupying the rest of Czechoslovakia later.

4. Only appeasement can succeed, either because the defender lacks the capability or will or both to mount a robust deterrence effort or, if war breaks out, to pursue it effectively. A possible example is what Barbara Tuchman regards as England's "missed opportunity" to appease and thereby retain its American colonies.[7]

Comparative studies of successful and unsuccessful appeasement can help identify the conditions under which appeasement may be a viable strategy, the risks of the strategy, and ways of coping with the risks. Such insights can be gained, for example, by comparing British appeasement policy toward Hitler with the gradual improvement in Anglo-French relations after the Fashoda crisis of 1898 and with Chancellor Willy Brandt's successful *Ostpolitik* policy toward the Soviet Union and Eastern Europe. Chamberlain's effort to employ appeasement as a tool for the larger objective of creating the conditions for a new structuring of peace and stability in Europe was, according to one interpretation, vitiated by his "impatience and contempt for the cautionary expedients of traditional diplomacy":

> While between 1933 and 1937, the British Foreign Office had sought, however imperfectly, to establish the bona fides of the dictators and to determine whether there were common interests and values that would serve as a basis for cooperation *before* undertaking a systematic removal of specific causes of conflict, Chamberlain saw no point in these preliminaries and soon got rid of those people, like Eden and Vansittart, who insisted on them. . . . [He] heedlessly plunged ahead to what should have been the final stage of a laborious process, on the mistaken assumption that Hitler and Mussolini shared his objectives and that a demonstration of his readiness to satisfy their demands would bring the peace that he desired.[8]

In contrast, Willy Brandt initiated his *Ostpolitik* policy with a clear notion not only of the changes he wished to achieve but also of the difficulties and risks that lay in his path. His policy embraced the possibility of making major concessions to the Soviet Union and the East German regime and, hence, certainly contained elements of appeasement. But Brandt skillfully employed the strategy of conditional reciprocity to orchestrate a complex process to ensure that he would gain the important benefits he sought in return. "Unlike Chamberlain in his dealings with Hitler, Brandt did not rush the . . . process in order to move as quickly as possible into appeasement." Rather, Brandt minimized and controlled the risks "by moving one step at a time and then waiting until the situation ripened before moving ahead again."[9]

A survey of the history of international relations should easily identify many other instances in which appeasement and conciliation either worked or did not, thereby enabling scholars to produce the conditional generalizations that will refine our understanding of when this strategy is and is not likely to be a viable one and how best to implement it.[10]

# 6. Why Deterrence and Reassurance Sometimes Fail

Few observers or policy officials would claim that the United States employed a robust version of deterrence strategy to dissuade Saddam Hussein from invading Kuwait. Although an authoritative, fully documented account remains to be written, the essential facts of the effort that began in mid-July 1990 have become well known and need not be related in detail here.[1]

After Saddam Hussein's bellicose speech on July 19, some administration officials saw the need to hurriedly improvise a strong deterrence effort. Efforts to do so, however, were diluted for various reasons and were further weakened by contradictory signals to Saddam from Washington. The administration did convey a general warning that it would defend its vital interests in the Gulf and would continue to support the sovereignty and integrity of the Gulf states. But it also stated that it would take no position on the issues dividing Iraq and Kuwait, thereby perhaps inadvertently signaling a willingness to appease Saddam's claims on Kuwait. Instead of giving Saddam Hussein a blunt and unequivocal statement that an invasion of Kuwait would be unacceptable and would be sharply resisted by ample force, as some Department of

Defense officials recommended, the administration issued equivocal statements about its commitment to Kuwait. While urging that Saddam's dispute with Kuwait be settled peacefully, Washington also stated more than once that the United States was not obligated by any treaty commitment to defend Kuwait with U.S. forces.

To the extent that Washington may have wanted to mount a stronger deterrence effort, it was dissuaded by Egypt and Saudi Arabia, which strongly enjoined the United States to stay out of the crisis with Iraq and offered assurances that the crisis could be resolved peacefully. The United Arab Emirates (UAE) took the possibility of military action by Iraq more seriously, however. In fact the UAE took the initiative in approaching Washington about a joint military exercise to serve as a deterrent signal to Saddam Hussein. When Washington publicized the exercise (a quite modest joint show of force), the UAE responded angrily because it had wanted the action to take place without publicity.

The failure of U.S. officials to mount a strong deterrence strategy cannot be attributed to an inadequate conceptual understanding on their part of the logic of deterrence and its general requirements. Policymakers knew that the strategy of deterrence requires communicating a threat so potent and credible in the opponent's (Saddam Hussein's) judgment that he will conclude that the probable costs and risks of moving against the victim (Kuwait) clearly outweigh the expected benefits. The explanation for the failure to mount a stronger deterrence effort in this case lies elsewhere. A number of circumstances and constraints made it extremely difficult for the administration to generate a credible and potent enough deterrent threat to overcome Saddam's strong motivation to act against Kuwait. Under the circumstances Saddam may well have regarded the United States as not really committed to respond to his move in a serious military way. An alternative explanation is that Saddam miscalculated not American but Arab reaction; believing that Arab governments would not allow American troops on their soil Saddam may have believed that, therefore, there could not be a strong U.S. military response to his move against Kuwait.

As in earlier historical cases—for example, the North Korean attack on South Korea in June 1950—when the aggressor judges a commitment to be lacking, the most rational strategy available to him for challenging the status quo is the fait accompli—the quick, decisive use of ample force to achieve the objective before the potential defender of the state subjected to attack can reconsider its policy and decide to intervene. And this is, indeed, the strategy of aggression Saddam chose to follow.[2]

Even at the time, it was clear that Washington faced difficult obstacles in trying to mount a stronger deterrence effort. As a senior administration official later explained to reporters, "We were reluctant to draw a line in the sand." Continuing, he added that one could not envisage at the time that the American public and Congress would support the deployment of substantial American military force for deterrence purposes over a dispute involving twenty miles of desert territory. Besides, it was clear that the local Arab states, in particular Saudi Arabia, would not have allowed the stationing of U.S. troops on their territory to deter an attack on Kuwait— all the more so, because Saudi leaders did not believe it would occur. And, as the senior official went on to point out, the administration did not wish to risk asserting a deterrent threat it was unprepared or unable to carry out if its bluff were called: "The basic principle is not to make threats you can't deliver on. That was one reason why there was a certain degree of hedging on what was said."[3] This case, then, illustrates some fundamental difficulties that can be encountered in efforts to employ deterrence strategy.

The lesson is a sobering one and points to the limitations of deterrence strategy. What the United States was willing and able to do *after* the aggression against Kuwait, it was not able to threaten to do on behalf of deterrence *before* the invasion occurred. It would be unjustified to read history backward, as critics are wont to do, and argue that the administration should have been able and willing to threaten on behalf of deterrence what it was able and willing to do to oppose the aggression after it occurred.

The present case illustrates once again a lesson that emerged from earlier studies calling attention to the limitations of deterrence strategy as an instrument of foreign policy. Deterrence cannot be counted on to compensate for a flawed foreign policy based on erroneous assumptions, such as the administration's prewar policy toward Saddam. A major power such as the United States, with its complex bureaucracy and decision-making process, cannot quickly or easily reverse direction and quickly improvise a strategy of deterrence when the adversary suddenly and unexpectedly poses the threat of aggression. Once a policy is established toward another state it acquires a momentum of its own that cannot be easily reversed. As a number of observers have noted, the Bush administration's response to the July crisis in the Gulf was influenced by its long-standing policy of developing better relations with Hussein's Iraq. Prior to the July crisis the administration was operating on the premise that the best way to handle Saddam and moderate his behavior was through offering conditional incentives and an improvement in relations in return for his cooperation and good behavior. (Whether this policy was clearly and consistently conveyed is another matter.) In other words, the essence of the policy was an attempt to resocialize the outlaw Iraqi state and reform its leader. That policy was based on what turned out to be dubious assumptions about Saddam's aspirations, intentions, and mind-set—assumptions that were not subjected to critical examination until it was too late (see chapter 4).

Washington's sudden concern over Saddam's intentions in late July and its move toward deterrence did not succeed altogether in overcoming the momentum of its earlier policy. Even while signaling its weak deterrence effort, the administration added reassurances that it wanted to remain on friendly terms with Iraq. Such reassurances could only further dilute the already weak deterrence effort.

One is reminded of the equally misguided reliance on reassurances of friendship that President Harry Truman and Secretary of State Dean Acheson conveyed to China in the autumn of 1950 when the Chinese leaders threatened to intervene in the Korean War if U.S. forces pursued the defeated North Korean forces beyond the thirty-eighth parallel into North Korea.[4] In employing deterrence, a correct image of the adversary's behavioral patterns is often critically important. The adversary's mind-set and calculations are not easily or reliably accessible. We can illustrate this point by briefly considering two scenarios (both drawn from historical cases), elements of which may apply also to Saddam's calculations leading to the attack on Kuwait.

In one scenario the adversary whom one is trying to deter may feel strong domestic or international pressure to act to change the status quo now. Such was President Nasser's situation in the crisis with Israel in 1967 when, according to one interpretation, he was pressed to move from one provocative action to another against Israeli security interests until, contrary to his wishes and expectations at the beginning of the crisis, the situation escalated to war. In this scenario, the adversary is led to take greater and greater risks, either knowingly or by unrealistically minimizing the risks. Deterring an adversary under these circumstances becomes appreciably more difficult, all the more so if the deterrer is not aware of the domestic and international pressures driving the adversary; the deterrer may assume incorrectly that the adversary is "rational" and that strong, credible deterrence is enough to induce prudence and caution.

In a second scenario the adversary may feel obliged to act against the status quo because he is operating with an exaggerated, even quite unrealistic, perception of the threat. The perception may be that the other state is considering or will soon consider hostile action or is certain to take aggressive action later on. In such a scenario, too, though for reasons other than those in the first scenario, the adversary may judge it necessary to take the substantial risk of initiating action himself instead of waiting for the other side to do so. Once again, deterrence becomes much more difficult even if the deterring state is aware, which is not always the case, of the accentuated threat assessment that is driving the adversary's behavior.

Something approximating this second scenario occurred during the Korean War, when in the late summer of 1950 Chinese leaders became alarmed at the implications of the U.S. decision to pursue the defeated North Korean forces into North Korea, occupy it, evict its Communist regime, and unify the two Koreas. Mao felt that if this were allowed to happen the United States would sooner or later take hostile action against mainland China and encourage the Chinese nationalist forces on Taiwan to do the same. Given this image of a hostile U.S. opponent, Mao decided it was preferable to take the considerable risks of intervening to evict U.S. forces from Korea than to face what he viewed as the greater risks and uncertainties of allowing North Korea to fall to the enemy. In a curious parallel to the Munich analogy, Mao reasoned that appeasing the United States now by accepting its occupation of North Korea should be ruled out because appeasement could only lead to a bigger and more dangerous war later.[5]

When the deterring state has reason to believe, as in the second of these two scenarios, that an adversary who may be contemplating military action has an exaggerated image of the deterrer's hostility and intentions, the question arises whether it is possible to reassure him that this is not the case. Is it possible to reduce his motivation to act, either by substituting reassurances for deterrence or by combining elements of both reassurance and deterrence? Although such an alternative policy appears promising, implementing it effectively is likely to be difficult in many situations. The possibility of coupling reassurance of some kind with deterrence, or substituting reassurance for deterrence, has only recently been highlighted by scholars.[6] One of their working hypotheses is that reassurance of some kind might be used instead of, or in addition to, deterrence when the adversary's motivation for acting against the status quo stems from a sense of weakness and vulnerability. Conversely, deterrence is thought to be more appropriate than reassurance when the adversary's motivation is derived not from his preoccupation with threat and vulnerability but from the belief that an opportunity exists for aggrandizement at acceptable cost and risk. These general hypotheses need elaboration and refinement that can be achieved only by careful comparative analysis of relevant historical experience.

I have already noted that in the several weeks before Iraq invaded Kuwait, U.S. policy employed weak variants of deterrence and reassurance. Reassurance was conveyed in signals to Saddam Hussein indicating a desire for continued friendship. The deterrence component of the U.S. response was quite weak and was perhaps further diluted by the effort to assure Saddam of the administration's desire for continuing friendly relations.

With the benefit of hindsight, several additional observations can be made regarding the difficulty and risks of resorting to reassurances in a situation of this kind. When the adversary who is contemplating aggression (Saddam Hussein) regards the deterring state as basically hostile and opposed to his "legitimate" foreign policy aspirations, he may misinterpret reassurances as an insincere effort to mask hostility. Such a response to reassurance is all the more likely if the adversary's mind-set is tainted with paranoia. (As is well known, paranoid personalities tend to be very suspicious of friendly gestures.) The adversary may also misinterpret efforts to reassure him as a sign of irresolution. This misinterpretation, in turn, may encourage him to question the credibility and significance of the deterrence directed toward him.

We cannot, and need not for present purposes, do more than call attention to the possibility that Saddam misinterpreted in one or another of these ways Washington's effort to reassure him. These possibilities are mentioned here to identify various risks and difficulties that may arise when reassurance is coupled with or substituted for deterrence of an adversary who, as Saddam evidently did, regards his opponent as basically hostile and certain in the long run to oppose the realization of his most important foreign policy aspirations.[7]

# 7. The Failure to Coerce Saddam Hussein

Some high-level U.S. policymakers and other foreign policy specialists were genuinely surprised that coercive diplomacy failed to persuade Saddam to withdraw his forces from Kuwait. Coercive diplomacy failed even though U.S. policymakers had a good conceptual understanding of the strategy and its requirements and acted accordingly. The explanation for the failure lies elsewhere, but the exact explanation cannot be easily determined. The answer lies buried in the values, beliefs, perceptions, and calculations that influenced Saddam Hussein's judgment and led to his decision to fight rather than accept the ultimatum of January 15, 1991.[1]

Before proceeding I will discuss the general concept of coercive diplomacy and indicate the limited though useful contribution it makes in helping policymakers devise a specific strategy that fits the particular situation at hand well enough to promise success. The general concept or model of coercive diplomacy identifies the major ingredients of the strategy and the logic that must be created in the mind of the adversary if it is to succeed. The general concept of coercive diplomacy becomes a strategy only when the policymaker gives specific content to the four components of coercive diplomacy. The policymaker must decide the following: (1) what to demand of the opponent; (2) whether—and how—to create in the adversary's mind a sense of urgency about complying with the demand; (3) how to create a threat of punishment for noncompliance that is sufficiently credible and potent in the adversary's mind to persuade him that compliance is more in his interest than facing the consequences; and (4) whether to couple the threatened punishment with positive inducements—a "carrot"—to make it easier for the adversary to comply. It should go without saying that the more far-reaching the demand, the stronger the opponent's motivation to resist and the more difficult the task of coercive diplomacy.

Depending on the policymaker's answers to these four questions, different variants of the strategy of coercive diplomacy are possible. The strongest is the ultimatum, either explicit or tacit, in which the demand on the opponent is accompanied by a deadline or a sense of urgency about compliance and is backed by a potent and credible threat of punishment for noncompliance. A weaker variant of coercive diplomacy is the gradual "turning of the screw," in which the sense of urgency about compliance is diluted, though not altogether absent, and the punishment threatened is not a single potent action but an incremental progression of increasingly severe pressure. Even weaker is the try-and-see variant of coercive diplomacy, in which the demand is accompanied by neither a sense of urgency about compliance nor a threat of punishment for noncompliance but, rather, is backed by a modest coercive threat or action, which, if ineffective, may be followed by another modest action or threat.

In the Gulf crisis, coercive diplomacy began with something approximating the gradual turning of the screw: increasingly severe economic sanctions. In late November 1990 this approach was replaced by the ultimatum form of the strategy backed by the threat of war. Well before taking this step, the Interagency Deputies Committee of the National

Security Council in early October carefully considered the utility and risks of subjecting Saddam to an ultimatum. (Evidently, therefore, the possibility of replacing sanctions with an ultimatum was a serious option at an early stage in the development of the crisis.) Drawing on historical experience (i.e., what I refer to elsewhere in this study as generic knowledge), the group appears to have identified four possible risks of an ultimatum:

1. The opponent may think you are bluffing.

2. The opponent may take the ultimatum seriously but decide to initiate war himself rather than accept the demand made on him (as the Japanese did in deciding to initiate war against the United States in December 1941).

3. The opponent may reject the ultimatum because he regards acceptance of it as humiliating, incompatible with honor, too damaging politically, and the like.

4. The opponent may neither accept nor reject the ultimatum outright but try to defuse its coercive impact by accepting the demands partially or with qualifications.

This working group undertook the difficult task of estimating whether any of these risks was likely to materialize if an ultimatum were employed against Saddam and how these risks might be minimized, if not avoided altogether. To this end, area experts were consulted. The full results of the group's analysis have not been made available for this study.[2] It appears that the major concern of policymakers at first was to make the threat of punishment so credible that Saddam would be extremely unlikely to regard it as a bluff. At the same time it appears that the working group was sensitive to the possibility that too explicit and harsh an ultimatum might harden his resistance; accordingly, an effort was made to give coercive diplomacy the character of a game of "chicken" that would last for some time. Later, however, as the January 15 deadline for compliance approached, the fourth risk of using ultimatums became a significant concern for the administration. The possibility that Saddam might announce partial or conditional withdrawal from Kuwait was referred to by well-informed journalists as the administration's "nightmare scenario." Very detailed contingency plans were made to deal with such a development and were discussed with coalition partners.

The prior question, of course, was why the administration considered it necessary to move from economic sanctions to a tough ultimatum backed by the threat of war. This decision was made not only because of the difficulty of making reliable intelligence estimates of the effect of sanctions on Iraq's economy (see chapter 3). In addition, there was concern that sanctions would take too long and might not be effective, and that it might be difficult to maintain the international coalition over a long period of time. Pressure to bring the crisis to a head quickly was encouraged by knowledge that weather conditions during the forthcoming summer would make combat difficult. Also, there was considerable pressure from Saudi Arabia to move to a threat of military action. Finally, the rationale for shifting to the ultimatum was strongly supported by personality assessments of Saddam Hussein that encouraged the belief that only an ultimatum backed by the threat of war had a chance of impressing him with the need to back down.

However, not all U.S. policymakers were sanguine that coercive diplomacy would be successful.[3] Besides, some members of the administration believed that success in coercing Saddam Hussein to withdraw from Kuwait would be an unsatisfactory outcome to the crisis: it would leave him in power, his military forces intact, and Iraq free to pursue its military programs for development of weapons of mass destruction. From this standpoint, failure of coercive diplomacy could be countenanced in that it would provide an opportunity to use military force to remove Saddam from power, destroy his military forces, and end Iraq's weapons development programs.

Let us consider more closely the image of Saddam held by

some American policymakers, which led them to believe that coercive diplomacy might well succeed but that the strongest form of the strategy would have to be applied. Psychological profiles of the Iraqi leader based on studies of his past behavior and attitudes indicated that while he was indeed dangerous and prone to take risks, he was by no means a martyr. Rather, the key to his survival in power for more than twenty years had been a capacity to reverse course when events indicated that he had miscalculated and was endangered. It was believed he could be coerced into retreating from Kuwait, but only if he were taken to the very brink of a devastating, all-out war and deprived of any alternative except the stark choice of backing down. In addition, as one of the assessments of Saddam emphasized, he would reverse himself only if he concluded that he could not otherwise survive in power and believed that by retreating he could preserve his power base.[4]

These conditions for persuading Saddam that it was in his interest to withdraw from Kuwait appeared to have been met as the January 15 deadline approached. Although the Bush administration, backed by the UN Security Council, refused to offer a formal carrot to make it easier for Saddam to back down, insisting there could be "no reward for aggression," it did convey several assurances that Saddam could have used for face-saving purposes had he decided to pull Iraqi forces from Kuwait. On several occasions administration leaders had stated that Iraq would not be attacked if it evacuated Kuwait, an assurance that presumably also guaranteed that vulnerable Iraqi forces exiting from Kuwait would be granted safe passage back to Iraq. Washington had also conveyed that it would not leave military forces in the Gulf after a peaceful resolution of the crisis. And, although Washington rejected the direct, formal linkage that Saddam had demanded between withdrawal of Iraq's forces and a Middle East peace conference, it did convey its expectation that a conference of this kind was possible, even likely, if Iraq withdrew from

Kuwait. Therefore, though not necessarily with much enthusiasm on the part of some administration leaders, the door was left open for Saddam to retreat back into Iraq, ensuring his survival in power without having to endure a war.

Why, then, did coercive diplomacy not work and war become necessary? Why did Saddam persist in his confrontational course in the face of the overwhelming military forces arrayed against him? Was the profile of him on which the policy of coercive diplomacy had been based incorrect? Or had Saddam been insufficiently impressed with the credibility and potency of the threat of war? In other words, had he miscalculated?

The latter explanation was favored by some of those who had subscribed to the view that Saddam was capable of retreat in the interest of political survival. One of these persons was Dennis Ross, the head of policy planning in the State Department. In an interview with a *Washington Post* journalist in October 1991, Ross offered the following explanation for the failure of coercive diplomacy:

> What I underestimated was his [Saddam Hussein's] perception of our resolve. He just didn't believe us. He had watched CNN . . . and his concept of the [congressional] debate was that it was a sign of weakness. Debate and dissent meant that we would fall victim the same way we fell victim in Lebanon and the same way we did in Vietnam.

> In this case, coercive diplomacy didn't work [also] because we could not convince him of what it meant to use force. He thought we were going to be hamstrung domestically. . . . The reality of what war meant for him didn't sink in until after the bombing [started in January].[5]

A more complex explanation was offered by Jerrold M. Post, M.D., a specialist on the psychology of political leaders and author of one of the earlier profiles of Saddam to which reference has already been made. Agreeing that Saddam had probably miscalculated the credibility and potency of the threat of war, Post added that cultural factors had probably contributed to such miscalculations. "In the Arab world," Post observed, "having the courage to fight a superior foe can bring political victory, even through a military defeat. . . ."

Post also suggests that the dynamics of the crisis may have led to an inflation of Saddam's heroic self-image: "Intoxicated by the elixir of power and the acclaim of the Palestinians and the radical Arab masses, Saddam may well have been on a euphoric high and optimistically overestimated his chances for success." Moreover, by publicly committing himself during the crisis to the Palestinian cause, thereby gaining widespread approval in the Arab world and enhancing his self-image, Saddam may have painted himself into a psychological corner. It became difficult thereafter to retreat without dishonor. According to this interpretation, Saddam thereby lost the capacity he had demonstrated on many previous occasions to retreat when necessary.[6]

A number of conclusions and lessons can be drawn from the failure of coercive diplomacy on this occasion. The case illustrates the importance of having an accurate profile of the adversary toward whom coercive pressure is directed. Ironically, however, it also illustrates at the same time the difficulty of fine-tuning the strategy so as to activate precisely that facet of the adversary's makeup that would ensure the desired response. Even when an insightful, sophisticated psychological model of the adversary is available, is supplemented by a knowledge of the adversary's political culture and political system, and is used appropriately in policymaking, there can be no guarantee of success. The adversary's reluctance to undertake a humiliating, costly retreat (one of the risks of an ultimatum referred to earlier) can activate psychological tendencies in him to look for indications that the threat is not credible or that the coercing state lacks the political will to engage in a costly war. Similarly, if the adversary falls prone to the familiar tendency toward wishful thinking his estimate of the relative military strength of the two sides will be distorted. As cognitive psychology has repeatedly and persuasively emphasized, a person tends to give greater, often uncritical weight to new information that supports an existing policy or preference and tends to discount evidence that challenges his existing mind-set. As a result, the adversary may make critical miscalculations that feed on his distaste for drawing the conclusion that it is really in his best interest to meet the demands made on him. Such miscalculations can be abetted if the adversary's mind-set includes, as Saddam's evidently did, an image of the coercing state as lacking the political will to engage in a tough battle in which it would have to take heavy casualties.

The failure of coercive diplomacy in the Gulf crisis also calls attention to the impact the adversary's self-image can have on his calculations and judgment when he is forced to decide whether to meet the demands made on him. That Saddam entertained an inflated image of himself as a heroic leader destined to transform the Arab world was known to those who have studied him. What was not anticipated, Post suggests, is that Saddam's self-image may have been so magnified by developments during the crisis that retreating became more difficult for him.

In sum, the lesson is that the outcome of coercive diplomacy may depend on psychological, cultural, and political variables operating on the adversary, which may be difficult to foresee and difficult to deal with to ensure the success of the strategy.

The Gulf crisis was a tough case for coercive diplomacy for a number of other reasons as well. These reasons emerge sharply in a comparison of the Gulf crisis, in which the strategy failed, with the Cuban missile crisis, in which it succeeded (see table 7.1). In the missile crisis Kennedy and Khrushchev could cooperate to avoid war because neither leader believed that their disagreement approximated a zero-sum contest, and because their image of war, should it occur, was that of a nuclear catastrophe. In contrast, President Bush and Sad-

**Table 7.1.** Six Variables That Help Explain Success or Failure of Coercive Diplomacy.

| Variables That Favor Success of Coercive Diplomacy | Cuban Missile Crisis | Gulf Crisis |
|---|:---:|:---:|
| Non-zero-sum view of the conflict | + | − |
| Overwhelmingly negative image of war | + | − |
| Carrot as well as stick | + | − |
| Asymmetry of motivation favoring state employing coercive diplomacy | + | − |
| Opponent's fear of unacceptable "punishment" for noncompliance | + | − |
| No significant misperceptions or miscalculations | + | − |

"+" = variable present; "−" = variable absent.

dam Hussein tended to see their conflict in zero-sum terms, and this tendency was reinforced by the highly invidious image each had of the other. Moreover, unlike Kennedy and Khrushchev, who were horrified by the possibility that, if mismanaged, the crisis could lead to thermonuclear war, Bush and Saddam held an image of the outcome, costs, and consequences of war that was not distasteful enough to motivate them to seek a compromise settlement. Incentives for cooperating to avoid war were lacking on both sides. Indeed, it is not far-fetched to characterize the Bush administration's policy as coercive diplomacy without fear of the consequences of failure.

In the Cuban crisis, moreover, Kennedy coupled his ultimatum with a substantial carrot: an agreement not to invade Cuba and a secret agreement to remove the U.S. Jupiter missiles from Turkey. In the Gulf crisis Bush relied solely on the "stick" and offered no carrot for a compromise settlement, insisting that there be no reward for aggression, although the ingredients for face saving were available to Saddam. In the

Cuban crisis, in contrast to the Gulf crisis, neither side had any significant misperceptions or miscalculations during the crisis that might have led to war. In the Cuban crisis, again unlike the Gulf case, Kennedy operated with an image of Khrushchev as a leader who was capable of retreating, which he was able to capitalize on in orchestrating an effective carrot-and-stick variant of the ultimatum.

Two other psychological variables that appear to have been important in past cases of coercive diplomacy were not present in the Gulf crisis. First, Kennedy succeeded in impressing Khrushchev that getting the missiles out of Cuba was more important to the United States than keeping the missiles there was to the Soviet Union. Evidently Bush did not succeed, despite considerable efforts, to convince Saddam that getting Iraqi forces out of Kuwait was more important to the United States than refusing to remove them under threat of war was to Iraq. Second, Kennedy created fear of unacceptable escalation of the crisis in Khrushchev's mind, but Bush did not succeed in creating fear of unacceptable punishment in Saddam's mind for noncompliance with the ultimatum.[7]

A final comment on the experience with coercive diplomacy in the Gulf crisis seems appropriate. The administration's willingness to contemplate use of force was a factor from an early stage in the crisis, when President Bush stated that Iraqi occupation of Kuwait was unacceptable. Thereafter, American policy was driven as much by the objective of creating and maintaining an international coalition under the aegis of the UN Security Council as it was by the desire to persuade Saddam Hussein to withdraw from Kuwait, if not more. Although the strategy of coercive diplomacy had little chance of success, the attempt to employ it in the hope of avoiding war was necessary for building and maintaining international and domestic support for the objective of liberating Kuwait. Ironically, the failure of coercive diplomacy was necessary to gain support for war when war became the last resort.

# 8. War Termination: Integrating Military and Political Objectives

The ending of the Gulf War constitutes an unusual, in some ways a unique, case of war termination. In some respects it resembles the ending of the war with Nazi Germany and Japan: the enemy was decisively defeated, and terms for a cease-fire were not negotiated with, but imposed on, the adversary. But the terms imposed on Iraq, unlike those for Germany and Japan, were not those of unconditional surrender, military occupation of the entire country, and replacement of the existing regime with a military government. Rather, for various reasons the United States was determined to avoid too much involvement in postwar Iraq. Though the UN coalition's military and political war aims in the Gulf War were extensive, they were limited in comparison with the terms imposed on Germany and Japan.

General theory and knowledge about war termination have been slow to emerge from scholarly studies. This deficiency in scholarship is largely due to the fact that there are many different types of war, different types of cease-fires, and different types of war termination.[1] One might add that in wars that end in military success for one side, the type of postwar relationship the victorious power wishes to develop with the defeated enemy varies greatly, ranging from a Carthaginian peace to weaken the enemy drastically so that it will not constitute a serious threat in the foreseeable future, to a "peace with honor" that does not unduly weaken the adversary and paves the way for early reestablishment of normal or friendly relations or even an alliance against other powers. In the Gulf War the UN coalition desired a postwar relationship with a weakened Iraqi state, preferably no longer led by Saddam Hussein but capable of remaining intact.

War should indeed be regarded, as Clausewitz emphasized, as a continuation of politics by other means. But the task of selecting military objectives that, if achieved, will facilitate achievement of broader political war aims has repeatedly encountered a variety of difficulties leading to disappointment with war outcomes, frustration, and acute controversy. Paradoxically, it appears easier to use overwhelming military force to achieve the very ambitious political goals of a total war than to achieve the more modest political objectives of a limited war. In some limited conflicts, even a resounding battlefield success cannot be easily converted into a wholly satisfactory political outcome.[2]

The Gulf War exemplifies the problem of war termination in some important respects. Questions may be raised about how well administration war planners were able to integrate military objectives and military strategy with the political war aims they hoped to accomplish, in particular the desire to find a way of removing Saddam from power. In addition, one may ask why intelligence failed to anticipate the Kurdish and Shi'ite rebellions that erupted shortly after the cease-fire of February 28, 1991, and whether better intelligence might have led to a more effective policy toward these important dissident groups both before and after the uprisings. Finally, granted that the post-Vietnam U.S. military doctrine demonstrated its merits in the Gulf War, did its insistence that force be employed only on behalf of well-defined military objectives constrain the possibility of more effective use of force to achieve political objectives?

To be sure, the allied coalition in the Gulf War was resoundingly successful in achieving all of its military objectives. Kuwait was liberated, the Iraqi army was routed, Iraq's military capability and its infrastructure were greatly weakened. Achievement of these military objectives also accomplished the most important of the allied coalition's political objectives. Thus, the regional threat posed by Iraq's powerful military forces was sharply reduced. And the general objective of establishing peace and security in the Middle East—called for by Security Council Resolution 678 of November 29, 1990, which had authorized use of force to liberate Kuwait—was furthered by stiff cease-fire terms that imposed on Iraq the obligation to destroy all nuclear, chemical, and biological weapons and production facilities as well as missiles capable of reaching the territory of other countries in the region. Iraq was obliged to accept and cooperate with UN efforts to identify all such capabilities and to monitor and carry out their destruction. (Because it is beyond the scope of this study I will not discuss the difficulties that had to be overcome in implementing these terms.)

However, an important political objective—the removal of Saddam Hussein from power—was not accomplished. To be sure, this objective was not explicitly authorized by the Security Council. Nor was it an official military objective of the Bush administration. That is, it was not among the military objectives formally assigned to General Schwarzkopf's forces; accordingly, military strategy did not include pursuit, capture, or elimination of the Iraqi leader.

Nonetheless, there can be no question that Saddam's ouster was keenly desired by the Bush administration. During the war, Washington urged the people of Iraq to force the dictator out, a theme purveyed also in psychological warfare. Although Saddam's arrest or removal was not made a condition for a cease-fire, the cease-fire provisions were designed not only to achieve the other political-military objectives already mentioned but also to maintain pressure for Saddam's overthrow. Washington frequently hinted that Iraq's punishment would be gentler and its recovery quicker if Saddam were replaced.[3] And the administration made last-minute efforts before the cease-fire of February 28 to use two specially prepared deep-penetration bombs to "get" Saddam in one of his hardened bunkers.[4]

As time passed after the end of the war, the administration's failure to eliminate Saddam became a major source of political criticism at home. In part, such criticism was strengthened by expectations that had been created by President Bush's earlier efforts to galvanize domestic support for the war by depicting Saddam as another Hitler. Not only was Washington criticized for having stopped the war before securing Saddam's removal, it was also criticized for standing by and allowing Saddam's forces to put down the Kurdish and Shi'ite rebellions that quickly erupted after the cease-fire.

Difficulties in integrating military objectives and political objectives arise particularly in limited wars—such as Korea, Vietnam, and the Gulf—rather than in total wars such as those waged against Nazi Germany and Japan. By definition, limited wars are fought for limited objectives, which in turn are pursued by limited military means.

In some limited wars, political leaders impose constraints that prevent military leaders from using optimal military strategy and tactics, and the result may be a gap between military strategy and political objectives. The Gulf War did not exhibit this particular difficulty, since the much-criticized decision to declare a cease-fire before U.S. troops completed the envelopment of Basra was not really consequential for achievement of war aims. As a result, it is true, some Iraqi forces escaped and could participate later in quelling the Shi'ite rebellion, but that outcome was not inconsistent with the UN coalition's limited political war aims. Besides, some five hundred thousand additional Iraqi troops remained relatively undamaged in northern Iraq.[5]

In undertaking to end the Gulf War, U.S. policymakers had to be sensitive to its idiosyncratic features, but they were not able to anticipate and master all of them. Indeed, policy planners were aware that many difficulties could arise in terminating the war against Iraq and began serious contingency planning for war termination as soon as the war began. They were aware, for example, of the classic difficulties and risks associated with cease-fires. But they did not anticipate the rebellions of the Kurds and Shi'ites almost immediately after the temporary cease-fire was declared on February 28 and the difficult problems and dilemmas these developments would create. Two questions therefore arise. Why did not the victorious allied armies pursue their advance into Iraq all the way to Baghdad to ensure the removal of Saddam from power? And why did not allied forces intervene to prevent the crushing of the Kurdish and Shi'ite rebellions?

The brief answer to these questions is that to do so would have required Washington and its allies to escalate the military and political objectives they had set for themselves. There were, in fact, important limitations to the political objectives. It is true that the UN coalition did intend to appreciably weaken Iraq militarily so that it would not constitute a threat to other states in the region. However, at the same time, it did not wish to weaken Iraq to the point of being unable to resist pressures from Iran and Syria. Rather, although a much-weakened Iraq would emerge from the war, it should be capable of contributing to maintaining a regional balance of power.[6]

Accordingly, the UN coalition did not seek—in fact, it wished to avoid—a breakup of the existing Iraqi state into several small entities or a Lebanonization of the internal situation within the country. For that reason, Washington's attitude was ambivalent toward the Shi'ite and Kurdish rebellions. This development, unexpected in war termination planning, created severe policy dilemmas for the United States and the UN coalition. The rebellions were welcomed insofar as they might contribute to undermining Saddam's ability to stay in power, but if they were too successful they might set into motion the disintegration of Iraq and trigger possible moves into parts of Iraqi territory by Iranian, Syrian, and Turkish forces. The United States was not willing to do much to influence the outcome of the rebellions.

The policy dilemma created by the rebellions for Washington was compounded by their effect on the role the UN coalition hoped the Iraqi military would play in unseating Saddam. Now, quite unexpectedly, the Iraqi military had the difficult task of repressing large-scale rebellions in both the north and the south. Washington and its allies believed they had no choice but to accept the Iraqi military's fierce efforts, under Saddam's command, to suppress the rebellions. The alternative, as they saw it, was to accept the possibility that the rebellions would lead to a disintegration of the country that would be highly inconsistent with the allied coalition's political war aims. In other words, an unexpected and politically embarrassing convergence of interest in containing the rebellions emerged between the United States and Saddam. The rebellions and the need to suppress them gave Saddam a new lease on life.

The rebellions also complicated and undermined for the time being any possibility that elements of the Iraqi military might move, as had been hoped, against Saddam. The unstable internal situation in Iraq also discouraged the United States from offering additional incentives to the Iraqi military and the Ba'thist party to move against Saddam. Although the Iraqi military had to be denounced for its activity against the rebels and punished for violating the cease-fire prohibition on use of fixed-wing aircraft, Washington was basically unwilling to stand in the way of the efforts the Iraqi armed forces were making to contain the rebellions at least well enough to prevent disintegration of the state. As for the Iraqi military, the priority task was to hold the country together; launching a coup that might result in a clash with forces loyal to Saddam was presumably all the more difficult.

A much more important constraint on U.S. military intervention on behalf of the rebellions was the strong reluctance of U.S. military and political leaders to become embroiled in the internal affairs of the defeated country. Earlier, Washington had come to a firm, well-considered decision not to undertake a prolonged occupation of Iraq territory or to accept any responsibility for its administration after the war ended. After the cease-fire, in response to criticism for not intervening on behalf of the rebellions, administration officials underscored and defended the policy. As White House spokesman Marlin Fitzwater put it, "We don't intend to involve ourselves in the internal conflict in Iraq."[7] One of Bush's advisers reminded the critics that "our mission was to liberate Kuwait, not to reform Iraq. We had no intention of getting bogged down in that mess." When criticized for not shooting down Iraqi helicopters that were attacking the rebels, General Powell and other administration officials minimized the importance of the helicopters; they argued that not only would shooting them down not do much good but (reflecting the fear of taking the first step on a slippery slope) afterward there would be pressure to go after Saddam's tanks and other forces.[8]

The administration's refusal to escalate its political and military objectives was not a purely ad hoc judgment in response to the unexpected turn of events. Rather, the decision to strictly limit its objectives and the scope of its military strategy, and to remove U.S. forces from Iraq as soon as possible, had been made much earlier. Some administration officials had been influenced in this direction by their memory of the Korean War, when the Truman administration, after achieving its objective of evicting North Korean forces from South Korea, escalated its war aim to unification of the two Koreas by force and adopted the ambitious and risky military strategy

of moving into North Korea to liquidate the Communist government in Pyongyang. Flushed with its success in defeating
the North Korean army, the Truman administration suc-
cumbed to the temptation and pressure to shift from a limited to a total war against Communist North Korea, where-
upon the Chinese intervened and the United States found
itself plunged into a prolonged and costly war. In the Gulf
crisis the situation differed, but the weight of the historical analogy was felt and reinforced the other major political-
diplomatic constraints that argued for hewing to the limited
political and military objectives the UN Security Council had
authorized instead of seeking support for broadening them.

As for the idea of sending U.S. forces all the way to Baghdad in the hope that doing so might lead to Saddam's ouster,
this military option had been considered in the administration's war planning and had been firmly rejected.[9] This judgment, too, was strongly influenced by the U.S. post-Vietnam
military doctrine that warned against military intervention on
behalf of ambitious, amorphous political objectives. According to the doctrine, force should be used only for achieving
strictly military objectives and it should be employed in ac-
cord with professional military judgment. The United States
should avoid becoming involved militarily in situations in
which it could not be successful in a relatively short time with
minimal casualties. To send ground forces to Baghdad, it was
believed, would entail substantial political and military risks
of that kind.

In late February, after coalition forces had routed the Iraqi
army in the Kuwait theater and in southern Iraq, going on to
Baghdad to get rid of Saddam and perhaps overthrow the
regime would have been possible from a military standpoint
but might well have resulted in substantial U.S. casualties and
a prolonged involvement of American forces in a highly unstable, volatile internal situation. (Relevant is the fact that
approximately one-half million Iraqi troops, including a

number of Republican Guard divisions based in northern Iraq, had thus far suffered little damage.)

This is not to imply that top civilian leaders in the Bush administration wanted deeper involvement and had to be dissuaded by the military chiefs. Most civilian leaders evidently shared their inhibitions and, also for broader political and diplomatic reasons, were strongly determined to minimize U.S. involvement in postwar Iraq. Domestic political support for the war was geared to limited military objectives and might erode rapidly if Washington embarked on more ambitious goals. Nor could UN and coalition support for a more far-reaching military campaign be counted on.

Besides, when the cease-fire was declared on February 28 further military action to bring about Saddam's downfall seemed unnecessary. It was widely believed within the administration and elsewhere that Saddam could not survive in power after suffering so savage and humiliating a defeat; the devastating war would surely weaken Saddam's control over his military and his other instruments of repression so that the encouragement given by the UN coalition to get rid of him would bring about the desired result within a reasonably short time. If Saddam survived for the time being, pressure to remove him would be enhanced by postwar continuation of the stiff economic sanctions against Iraq.

Could the administration have acted more effectively to ensure Saddam's downfall and to cope with the policy dilemmas created by the rebellions? Critics of the administration's decision to halt the war "prematurely" benefit, of course, from hindsight, and it can be said that they either do not understand or do not give enough weight to the considerations that led Washington to limit its political and military objectives. For some critics it would have been preferable to discourage or (if necessary) prevent the Iraqi army from repressing the rebellions and to accept the possibility that Iraq might break up into several entities. Other critics argue that the coalition forces should have continued on to Baghdad—perhaps to surround and lay siege to it rather than to occupy it—in the hope that such a move would trigger a coup against Saddam, his death, or even his flight and the creation of a new government. We have already reviewed the grounds on which this military option was rejected by the administration.

However, a lesser option, with fewer of the disadvantages and risks of a march to Baghdad, was available. It was discussed within the administration in early March and rejected for many of the same reasons. The proposal, which originated with members of a high-level interagency committee, was that allied forces remain indefinitely in southern Iraq, a fairly lightly populated area under which lay most of Iraq's oil fields. The object would be not only to put pressure on the Iraqi government to comply with cease-fire terms but also to encourage efforts to remove Saddam. U.S. military chiefs are said to have voiced strong and decisive opposition to the proposal. For them, as well as for some civilian officials, it was enough that all the military objectives of the war had been fully accomplished. To keep U.S. forces in Iraq might well be the first step toward prolonged involvement of American forces in a highly unstable, volatile internal situation in Iraq. From this perspective, once the military objectives of the war were accomplished it was best to pull U.S. forces out of Iraq as soon as possible.

These controversies over the termination of the Gulf War have been briefly noted without an effort to evaluate either the desirability or the feasibility of the alternatives critics argue should have been pursued. In all likelihood, however, historians of the Gulf War will address the following questions in some depth with greater perspective and, of course, with fuller access to relevant data. First, was it wise to stop the war before securing Saddam's removal? Consideration of this question is likely to focus less on the option of authorizing coalition forces to go to Baghdad than on the more limited option of letting allied forces remain longer in southern Iraq to create additional pressure and leverage for Saddam's removal.

Second, did the conservatism of the post-Vietnam U.S. military doctrine, as manifested in its insistence that force be employed only to achieve strictly military objectives, unduly limit the possibility of more effective use of force and threats of force to achieve broader objectives in the Gulf War?

Third, why were U.S. and allied intelligence services unable to foresee the likelihood that after the defeat inflicted on Iraqi forces the Kurds and Shi'ites would rise in rebellion? Should Washington have established closer working relations with these groups during the early stages of the Gulf crisis? Since the administration had called on the people of Iraq to rise up against Saddam, did it not have a responsibility to protect the Kurdish and Shi'ite rebels?[10]

\* \* \* \*

Finally, a few general remarks that will perhaps provide a framework for considering the difficult question of integrating military and political objectives in limited conflicts of this kind. It is misleading and conceptually incorrect to pose the problem, as is often done, as a problem of matching military objectives and political objectives. Such a formulation assumes that—and begs the question whether—acceptable military means can always be devised that, if successful, will achieve the political objectives of a limited war. In fact, often there are political aims that cannot be realized solely via victory on the battlefield. Not only are there inescapable limits on the utility of force as an instrument of policy, but unforeseen consequences of military victory and unexpected developments thereafter—as in the Gulf War—can handicap the ability of even sophisticated statesmen to convert military victory into a full-blown political success. The achievement of political war aims in some conflicts, if indeed they are achievable to begin with, often requires diplomatic and other skills, but sometimes even these will not suffice.

In sum, military success may be a necessary condition for achieving ambitious political war aims, but it is not a sufficient condition for doing so. Other variables and unpredictable developments often come into play in the complicated "end game" that determines the political outcome of a limited war such as that in the Persian Gulf. In this war, as in some others, the end of the fighting begins a new phase in which the pursuit of some of the political objectives of the war continues. In planning for such a war the critical question is how, and to what extent, will a particular kind of military strategy empower the victor to achieve all of his postwar political objectives.

My purpose has been to identify and analyze problems of war termination, difficulties that are not easily anticipated or avoided. Analysis focused on the difficulty of converting battlefield success into full achievement of political war aims, a problem that frequently arises in war termination and that needs more systematic comparative study than it has thus far received.

# Concluding Note to Part Two

Part two has focused on critical developments in U.S policy toward Iraq from the end of its war with Iran in August 1988 through the termination of the Gulf War in late February 1991. At different points in this period the United States employed six different strategies toward Iraq. Five of the strategies proved to be unsuccessful and the other resulted in a mixed outcome.

My purpose has not been to write definitive, detailed histories of these efforts to influence Iraq or to contribute to political criticism of the administration for those of its strategies that were unsuccessful. Rather, my objective has been to provide analytical evaluation of the relationship of knowledge to action in the conduct of foreign policy. I have tried to implement this general objective by focusing on U.S. policy toward Iraq to show more concretely the relevance of conceptual and generic knowledge of strategies for the task of the policymaker.

Accordingly, in each of the preceding chapters I asked whether adequate theoretical conceptualization and generic knowledge in fact existed for each of these strategies on which policymakers might draw. My finding is that the state of systematic knowledge was altogether lacking or deficient for four of the strategies—resocialization of outlaw states and rogue leaders, appeasement, reassurance, and aspects of war termination. In the virtual absence of policy-relevant theory for these strategies, policymakers had no choice but to operate on the basis of their own inadequate conceptions of the strategies they were attempting to employ vis-à-vis Iraq. They lacked a systematic understanding of the conditions and requirements for the effective employment of these strategies. However, the reader will have noted that I have *not* attempted to argue that better knowledge of these strategies and a more accurate image of Saddam would surely have enabled U.S. policymakers to do better in dealing with him. Such counterfactual arguments of the "what if" kind are difficult to make persuasively. Instead, in the chapters dealing with these strategies I have been content to draw some provisional "lessons" and to offer suggestions for better conceptualization and understanding of the requirements for their effective use.

For the other two strategies—deterrence and coercive diplomacy—quite adequate conceptualization and general knowledge of their requirements have been available for a number of years. And it is reasonable to assume that policymakers were familiar with this knowledge and tried to make use of it to devise effective variants of deterrence and, later, coercive diplomacy against Iraq. These two strategies failed for other reasons. Chapter 6 called attention to one of the familiar limitations of deterrence as an instrument of diplomacy, namely, that in certain situations domestic, international, and situational constraints can severely hamper the ability of policymakers to improvise a strong variant of deterrence. The irony of the case, as in some earlier ones, is that what the United States and its allies were able to do in response to Iraq's aggression, they were not able to threaten to do in order to deter it!

The explanation for the failure of coercive diplomacy against Iraq is of quite a different order (see chapter 7). Unlike the weak variant of deterrence improvised in late July 1990, a very strong variant of coercive diplomacy was put together by the United States and its coalition partners. It failed for reasons that have largely to do with the way in which Saddam Hussein perceived the crisis and its stakes and calculated and miscalculated the outcome. The failure of coercive diplomacy in this case adds to and reinforces lessons derived from previous efforts to employ this strategy, some of which have succeeded and others of which have failed.

The three types of policy-relevant knowledge that were outlined in the Introduction have been alluded to in the foregoing analysis of the administration's strategies toward Iraq. These are (1) a general, abstract conceptualization of the strategy, (2) generalizations (or generic knowledge) about the conditions that favor the success of the strategy and the obstacles that it may encounter, and (3) actor-specific knowledge of the behavioral patterns of the adversary.

These types of knowledge are discussed in much greater detail in chapter 10, along with the contributions they are capable of making to policymaking. But first I believe it will be useful to discuss in chapter 9 the state of contemporary international relations theory in order to call attention to the limited contribution it makes to foreign policymaking.

The larger purpose of parts two and three is to emphasize that much work remains to be done to develop policy-relevant theory and knowledge about the many different strategies and instruments of diplomacy employed in the conduct of foreign policy. Adequate scholarly knowledge does not exist for many of these instruments of policy. And even when it does exist for particular strategies, more systematic understanding is needed of the problems of implementing them in different kinds of situations.

Part Three

**The Bridge between Knowledge and Action**

# 9. Contemporary International Relations Theory

In this chapter, I will discuss the state of international relations theory and comment on its uses and limitations from the standpoint of the knowledge requirements for conduct of foreign policy. Chapter 10 deals with other approaches that offer greater policy relevance, and the Summary and Conclusions contains general implications for scholarly research that aims at producing policy-relevant theories.

What, then, is the state of contemporary international relations theory and what does it contribute to the knowledge base for conducting foreign policy? Expectations in this respect should not be excessive, since, as is well known, theory necessarily abstracts and simplifies reality to some extent. Moreover, as we have been reminded by the difficulties scholars have encountered in trying to explain the failure to predict the end of the Cold War, theory must often struggle to catch up with changing realities; in the field of international relations, theory generally does better explaining what has happened than predicting what will happen.[1] For various reasons, therefore, we should not expect too much from general theories of international relations, for they do not attempt, and by no means claim, to provide all the knowledge needed for the conduct of foreign policy.

The study of international relations lacks a single comprehensive, coherent theory. Rather, theorizing is fragmented, much of it is not very well developed, and (no surprise) the field continues to be marked by often intense controversy. Much of the "Third Debate" currently being waged by international relations theorists is focused on epistemological and normative issues. Rarely do participants in this debate ask what difference the positions they advocate makes for the development of policy-relevant knowledge.[2] Indeed, many scholars in the field show little interest in bridging the gap between theory and practice. At the same time, however, other research on international relations theory is evolving in important directions as scholars pay increasing attention to developing knowledge that has policy relevance, broaden the agenda of problems to which theory should be applicable, and undertake more sophisticated and systematic study of the importance of cognitive, organizational, and political variables.[3]

The dominant academic theory of international politics—variously referred to as structural realism or sometimes neorealism—deals only with basic structural features of the international system: the "anarchical" nature of the system, the relative distribution of power, and the importance of the balance of power. This theory draws on the tradition of political realism, which has ancient roots in the writing of Thucydides, and attempts to transform classical realism into a scientific-deductive theory that focuses on the structure of the international system. The most authoritative and influential statement of neorealist theory is Kenneth Waltz's *Theory of International Politics*. It should be noted that Waltz's theory is a leaner version of the classical realist theory that was formulated many years ago by Hans Morgenthau. It avoids questionable assumptions, ambiguities, and contradictions that Waltz and other scholars discerned in Morgenthau's writings with respect to the central concepts of power, national interest, and balance of power.[4] At the same time, Waltz's book has stimulated a considerable debate regarding the uses and limitations of structural realist theory and numerous suggestions for broadening the scope of international relations theory.[5]

Classical realist theory was more comprehensive in scope and more ambitious in its aims than Waltz's leaner neorealist theory. Morgenthau, for example, claimed not only that his version of political realism could explain and predict the play of international politics but also that it could and ought to guide statesmen engaged in the conduct of foreign policy. In other words, Morgenthau's theory was also a theory of statecraft. In contrast, narrowing the scope of Morgenthau's theory, Waltz attempted to convert it into a scientifically respectable deductive theory, one that relies on structural attributes of the international system to generate predictions and provide a basis for explaining outcomes of international politics. We need to consider how well it achieves these goals and how much it contributes to the knowledge base that is necessary for conducting and understanding foreign policy.

Although cast in the form of a deductive theory, structural realism is not a full-fledged deductive theory, because its key variables and hypotheses have not been "operationalized" so that outcomes can be predicted in specific cases.[6] In consequence, structural realist theory can make only general, probabilistic predictions. But since such predictions lack grounding in systematic empirical analysis of the observed relationship between relative capabilities and outcomes in a large and presumably representative sample of interactions between states, the theory cannot express probability in statistical terms and is little more than a statement of likelihood. Nor does structural realism do much by way of identifying the conditions under which it expects its predictions to materialize. (See the discussion in chapter 10 about probabilistic predictions versus conditional predictions.)

As the theory's foremost proponents acknowledge, the few structural variables encompassed by the theory operate not as determinants of statesmen's choices of policy, but merely as constraints, though certainly important constraints, on those choices. In effect the theory warns that the relative power of states in the international system should be properly attended to by statesmen in conducting foreign policy, because their failure to respect the power advantage of an adversary will likely lead to their state being punished—either by being eliminated as an actor in the system or by incurring costly setbacks in interactions with other states. This general warning is indeed highly relevant and useful, but policymakers are still left to decide as best they can how, and by how much, their calculation of utility and risk should be influenced by power inferiority when they consider whether and how to pursue their interests in specific situations. And, as will be noted later, leaders of weak states—not deterred by the general warning conveyed by structural realism—often find strategies for advancing their interests in interactions with stronger states with some success.

Particularly relevant to this discussion of the relationship of knowledge to action, therefore, is the fact that structural realist (neorealist) theory is not a theory of foreign policy. This point was explicitly acknowledged by Waltz, who warned against expecting his theory to "explain the particular policies of states" and regarded it as an error "to mistake a theory of international politics for a theory of foreign policy." Waltz also acknowledged that structural realist theory "makes assumptions about the interests and motives of states, rather than explaining them." That he regards structural realism as a theory of constraints on foreign policy rather than a theory of foreign policy was made clear in the additional observation that "what it [structural realist theory] does explain are the constraints that confine all states."[7]

Although structural realist theory is not a theory of foreign policy, it is nonetheless useful for present purposes to identify its limitations from the standpoint of the knowledge base that is needed for the conduct of foreign policy. "Power" remains an elusive concept in the theory. The emphasis on the importance of the differences in power among states fails to take into account that not all the capabilities a state possesses come into play and influence the outcome of its interactions with other states. The theory fails to distinguish—and cannot distinguish—between what might be called the totality of *gross capabilities* a state possesses and the often much more limited *usable options* that its leaders can employ or wish to employ in particular situations. And yet the distinction between gross capabilities and usable options is often critical for understanding why powerful states do less well in military conflicts and trading disputes with weaker states than with stronger states.[8] Much of the power resources a strong state possesses may simply not be relevant or usable in some disputes with weaker states (or, indeed, with other powerful states). Weaker states often do surprisingly well in disputes with stronger states insofar as they enjoy asymmetry of motivation, a variable that can compensate for inferiority in overall power capabilities. What is at stake in a particular dispute may be more important to the weaker state than to its stronger rival; that is, the "balance of interests" may work to the advantage of the weaker state and enable it to obtain a better outcome than could be predicted by the relative distribution of raw power capabilities.

Thus, if it is true (as structural realist theory warns) that weaker states can be punished if they ignore power inferiority with strong states, it is also true (but structural realist theory fails to add) that strong states can be punished if they ignore the asymmetry of motivation that weaker states sometimes enjoy in disputes with stronger states. Nor should one overlook that strong states often have multiple, global foreign policy interests that compete with and place in perspective the particular interests involved in disputes with weaker states. The more powerful state may not attach enough importance to these particular interests to warrant a heavy expenditure of resources to achieve a maximum payoff in the dispute with a weaker but highly motivated adversary.

None of these limitations of structural realist theory is un-
known to or denied by scholars who attach great importance
to the theory. The sophistication of their understanding of
the complexities and uncertainties of international relations
is much broader than the scope of the theory. The point emphasized here concerns the theory itself; its inability to encompass the distinction between gross capabilities and usable
options is a major limitation. The deficiency is intrinsic to the
theory, not a missing piece that could be added without
changing the very nature of the theory's exclusive focus on
structural variables. Rather, the distinction between gross capabilities and usable options can be accommodated only by a
different kind of theory that works with the decision-making
level of analysis and studies the actual process of strategic interaction between states, both of which are deliberately excluded from structural realist theory.

Another major deficiency is the limited scope of structural
realist theory. Much that goes on in relations among states,
including what policymakers are sometimes most concerned
with, cannot be explained, predicted, or guided by the maxims of structural realist theory. Critics have pointed to a number of limitations of the scope of the theory, including that it
does not provide much help in addressing and understanding (1) all the sources of long-term trends in the international
system, (2) how to promote peaceful change in the international system, (3) how to avoid conflict and how to resolve it
via diplomacy, (4) how to achieve cooperation among states,
and (5) how to understand and promote foreign policy
"learning" by states and their leaders. Each of these important problems requires policymakers and students of foreign
policy to pay attention to variables that are excluded from
structural realist theory.

Still another limitation of structural realist theory is that
not only are its predictions sometimes badly off the mark,
which is to be expected of any theory that is capable of making only probabilistic predictions, but even its correct predic-

tions are typically very general. For example, although it is true that during World War II structural realist theory would have successfully predicted conflict developing between the United States and the Soviet Union after their cooperation in defeating Nazi Germany, the theory could not predict whether postwar U.S.-Soviet conflict would result in a spheres-of-influence agreement, a withdrawal of the United States from Europe in favor of a hemispheric "Fortress America" security policy, a relatively benign collaborative-competitive relationship, a cold war, or World War III. Other variables, not encompassed by structural realist theory, would have to be considered in order to try to predict or explain any of these highly different outcomes. Indeed, structural realist theory was not designed to make more specific predictions of this kind. I am not criticizing it for being unable to do more than it was designed to do but merely pointing out the important limits of what it is capable of doing when viewed from the perspective of the knowledge base needed for conducting and explaining important foreign policy outcomes.

In sum, although structural realist theory is an indispensable and necessary part of the knowledge needed, it is quite insufficient by itself for the study, and even more insufficient for the conduct and management, of international affairs. Other variables that influence foreign policy decisions and their outcomes but are not encompassed by structural realist theory—such as domestic structure and politics, ideology, belief systems, images of the opponent, bureaucratic politics, strategy and bargaining—need to be brought into the analytic framework. At the same time, of course, the substantial difficulty of developing theory and generalizations about how these additional variables also affect foreign policy decisions and outcomes must be recognized.

This discussion has used the critique of structural realist theory as an example. Other approaches to theory have similar or other limitations from a policy perspective. This particular theory has been used here to illustrate the general limitations of theories of international relations, because this one is currently predominant in academic circles.

How, then, can progress be made in developing the additional knowledge needed for the study and conduct of foreign policy? One approach that scholars have taken is to develop empirically derived generalizations about the ways in which *each* of these additional variables—domestic politics, bureaucratic politics, ideology and so on—influences the process of policymaking, the content of decisions, the implementation of policies, and their outcomes. Knowledge of this kind can indeed sensitize policy specialists, if they have not already been alerted through experience, to the ways in which foreign policy can be influenced for better or worse by each of these variables. However, theories and generalizations that focus narrowly on but one of these individual causal variables are of limited utility, among other reasons because they are not linked with variation in situational contexts and with strategies and instruments of policy that practitioners employ in attempting to influence outcomes in their interactions with other states. The discussion now turns to theories and knowledge about strategies, but first it should be acknowledged, as was noted in the Introduction, that policymakers need many other types of knowledge as well, for example, scholarly studies of global trends and problems.

# 10. Types of Knowledge for Policymaking

In chapter 9, I noted that the dominant theory of international relations, structural realism, is not a theory of foreign policy. Although realist theory identifies important constraints on statecraft, it provides limited guidance and very little of the knowledge required for the conduct of foreign policy. How, then, can progress be made in identifying and developing the additional knowledge base needed by policymakers for analyzing and dealing with the broad range of foreign policy tasks they are called on to discharge?

I will not attempt to provide a complete inventory of all the many different types of knowledge that can contribute to more effective policymaking. I will focus on substantive theories that deal with standard foreign policy undertakings—in particular, those that focus on strategies and undertakings that policymakers often resort to in dealing with adversaries. And I will leave aside "process theory," which focuses on ways of structuring and managing the policymaking system so as to increase the likelihood of selecting better policies.

## Substantive Theory and the Policymaking Process

It is difficult to ensure that relevant substantive knowledge will be brought to bear in policymaking, for three reasons.

One is that the policymaking process is often driven by internal and international political forces that squeeze out or limit the impact of relevant substantive knowledge. Indeed, for this reason some of those interviewed for this study expressed a sober view of the prospects for improving policymaking by developing and making available better knowledge of various types of foreign policy strategies and actions. However, one cannot demand assurance that relevant scholarly knowledge will be used in policymaking as a precondition for attempting to improve the knowledge base.

A second reason is that *general knowledge of international relations produced by scholars can only be an input to, not a substitute for, policy analysis of a specific problem conducted within the government.* Policy analysts, not academic scholars, have the difficult task of adapting the available general knowledge about a given strategy or a foreign policy undertaking to the particular case at hand. To do so, policy analysts must draw on available information about the particular case; such information comes from various intelligence and journalistic sources, not from bodies of theory or general knowledge of foreign affairs.

Third, *generic knowledge of a strategy or of a standard foreign policy undertaking is not a substitute for, but only an aid to, the final judgment of top policymakers.* The same generally can be said regarding the results of policy analysis; it, too, is an aid, not a substitute for the judgment of the top policymakers.[1] This is so because top policymakers typically must take into account factors such as domestic political considerations, international opinion, value priorities, and short-term versus long-term payoffs, which either were not considered by policy analysts or were not given the same weight that top policymakers assign to them.

It will be useful at this point to recall some of the observations made in chapter 2 about the policymaker's exercise of judgment. Whereas scholars and policy analysts can and should concern themselves with identifying a high-quality policy option, top policymakers have to deal with the difficult trade-off between doing what they can to enhance the quality of a policy and the need for obtaining sufficient consensus and support for the policy option they eventually choose. Also, top policymakers have to decide how much time and how much of the limited pool of resources to allocate to each of these efforts.

In other words, a distinction can be made between *effective* and *rational* decision making. Decision making is effective when the policymaker deals reasonably well with trade-offs between quality, support, and time and other resources. Rational decision making, on the other hand, reflects the scholar's and the policy analyst's effort to come up with a high-quality policy decision without reference to these trade-offs and the various political considerations with which the policymaker must deal. Although scholars have provided a number of models of rational decision making, there exists no theory of effective decision making that continues to rely upon ad hoc judgments by top policymakers.

\* \* \* \*

Three types of knowledge can help policymakers decide whether and how to employ a particular strategy. Scholarly studies by academics, research and intelligence specialists within the government, and other analysts are a major way of accumulating these types of knowledge: (1) An abstract conceptual model (or a quasi-deductive theory) of each strategy. (2) General (or "generic") knowledge of the conditions that favor the success of a strategy and, conversely, the conditions that make its success unlikely. (3) An actor-specific behavioral model of the adversary.

## Abstract Conceptual Models of Strategies

An abstract conceptual model of a strategy—such as deterrence, coercive diplomacy, crisis management, war termination, détente, appeasement, dispute resolution, or cooperation—identifies the critical variables of that strategy and the general logic that is associated with successful use of that instrument of policy. Let us take the relatively simple concept of deterrence to illustrate these points. The threat to respond to actions that an adversary may be thinking of taking against a state's interests is a critical variable of deterrence theory. A deterrence policy may specify the threatened actions or refer to them in a deliberately ambiguous manner. Similarly, the threatened response to such actions, should they occur, may be specified or left open. However, the logic of deterrence requires that the threat to respond to an action against a state's interests should be sufficiently credible and potent to persuade the adversary that the costs and risks of the action he is or may be contemplating outweigh the expected gains. The logic of this abstract deterrence model, therefore, rests on the general assumption that the opponent is rational and able to calculate his benefits, costs, and risks correctly.

Abstract conceptual models exist or can be formulated for other strategies as well. Two limitations of the usefulness of such models for policymaking should be noted. First, the abstract model is not itself a strategy but merely the starting point for constructing a strategy. The usefulness of an abstract model for policymaking is limited to providing the basic framework for understanding the general requirements for designing and implementing a strategy. The abstract model identifies only the general logic—that is, the desired impact on the adversary's calculations and behavior—that is needed for the strategy to be successful. But the abstract model does not indicate precisely what the policymaker has to do to induce that logic into the adversary's calculations. To achieve that result the policymaker has to tailor the abstract model into a specific strategy for the particular situation at hand and for the behavioral characteristics of that particular adversary.

One example should indicate what needs to be done to move from an abstract conceptual model to a specific strategy. This example concerns coercive diplomacy, a strategy that relies on threats to induce an adversary to stop or undo a hostile action he is engaged in. To convert the abstract model of coercive diplomacy into a specific strategy the policymaker has to specify each of the four variable-components of the general model:

1. What demand to make on the opponent.
2. Whether and how to create a sense of urgency for compliance with the demand.
3. How to create and convey a threat of punishment for noncompliance that will be sufficiently credible and potent to persuade the adversary that compliance is in his best interest.
4. Whether to couple the threat with a positive inducement (i.e., a "carrot") to make compliance easier for the adversary and, if so, what kind and how much of an inducement to convey.

These variable-components of the abstract model of coercive diplomacy may be likened to blank lines that the policymaker must fill in when designing a specific strategy of coercive diplomacy. (For further discussion of coercive diplomacy see chapter 7.)

The second limiting characteristic of abstract conceptual models for policymaking is that they are typically not full-fledged deductive theories. A fully developed deductive theory of deterrence or coercive diplomacy, if properly constructed, could be used to predict whether the strategy would succeed or fail in a particular situation. That contribution would be invaluable to policymakers, since it would remove uncertainty and guesswork. However, to have this capability the abstract model (which is, in effect, an incomplete or quasi-deductive theory) would have to be "operationalized"—that is, all its variable-components as well as the interaction among them would have to be capable of being specified and measured. Fully developed deductive theories of foreign policy strategies do not exist and will be difficult to develop. And it is by no means clear that even if a deductive theory could be adequately operationalized it would be able to predict the outcomes of efforts to employ the strategy.[2]

## Generic Knowledge of Conditions Favoring a Strategy

The limited contribution of abstract conceptual models can be compensated for somewhat by identifying conditions that, if present in a particular case, favor the success of a strategy. Generic knowledge of this kind can be obtained only by means of empirical research that systematically compares instances when the strategy succeeded with cases in which it failed. In doing so the investigator identifies variables and conditions that account for or explain the variance in the outcomes of the strategy. Research of this kind can be based either on a relatively small number of cases in which a variant of the method of historical explanation was used or by means of statistical analysis of a large number of cases.[3] Preferably both types of studies should be done as part of a broader, integrated research program. The cases studied can be historical instances in which the same strategy or various simulations of it were employed.

As this characterization of generic knowledge implies, such knowledge takes the form of *conditional generalizations* (or laws, as they are often referred to in discussions of theory). Generalizations are referred to as conditional when they identify factors that appear to have favored success of the strategy and other conditions that are associated with likely failure of the strategy. Such generalizations are most useful when they identify different causal patterns that lead to the success or failure of a strategy. Conditional generalizations are more useful in policymaking than generalizations that assert that a probabilistic relationship exists between two variables without identifying the conditions under which the relationship does and does not hold.

A brief comparison of conditional generalizations with

other forms that knowledge of the efficacy of a strategy can take is needed at this point. Ideally, one would like to discover universal, deterministic generalizations (or laws) that would tell us that whenever a particular condition or set of conditions is present the strategy will succeed. Such universal generalizations, taking the form "If A, then B," posit that the presence of condition A is sufficient for the occurrence of B. However, given the complexity of international relations phenomena, it is most unlikely that valid universal generalizations will be discovered either through empirical research or by developing full-fledged deductive theories.

We are somewhat more likely to discover a different type of relationship, one in which A is a necessary, but not a sufficient, condition for the occurrence of B. But attempted generalizations of this kind are fragile, since logically the discovery of only one case in which B occurred in the absence of A falsifies the proposition that A is a necessary condition for B's occurrence. Moreover, it is quite possible that a necessary condition actually contributes little to the causal explanation of the outcome. That is, the missing additional conditions may be much more important than the necessary one for the occurrence of B.

In any case, available research indicates that the outcomes of strategies are sensitive to many conditions and that no single causal pattern explains all successes and no single causal pattern explains all failures. Therefore, we need to go beyond the search for a single conditional generalization that can distinguish all successes from all failures—a quest that is not likely to be achieved—to developing conditional generalizations and causal patterns for different types of success and for different types of failures of a given strategy.

Given the complexity surrounding the phenomena we are interested in, it is sensible to set aside or at least play down the search for necessary or sufficient conditions. It is preferable instead to regard those conditions that do seem to have causal importance in explaining some successes of a strategy as *favoring conditions*. That is, the presence of these conditions in a particular case makes the strategy more likely to succeed. Similarly, the more favoring conditions in a case, the more likely is success. But favoring conditions are neither necessary nor sufficient for the success of a strategy.

This is not to say, however, that producing conditional generalizations is a relatively simple research task. For example, despite the considerable research effort of many scholars over the years who have addressed the question "Do arms races lead to war?" a recent review of this literature tells us that "there is still no well-developed theory that describes the circumstances under which arms races will or will not lead to war. Nor is there a theory that provides a reliable guide for policymakers."[4] However, what the cumulation of research on this question does permit us to say is not without value. It is clear that arms races are neither a *necessary* condition for the occurrence of war (since wars do sometimes occur in the absence of a prior arms race) nor a *sufficient* condition for war (since an arms race is not always followed by war). Given additional assessment of the relevant historical experience, it should be possible at the very least to identify a number of conditions that, if present in an arms race, can be said to favor or increase the likelihood of war. It may be hoped that such a study would also identify ways in which policymakers can act to reduce or control the likelihood that an arms race might result in war. I have not been able to discover a systematic study of this kind in the literature.

A few examples will illustrate the nature of conditional generalizations. Some years ago, after comparing a number of historical cases of successful and unsuccessful efforts to mediate conflicts, Zartman advanced a theory of *ripeness*, which identifies a number of conditions that, if present in a conflict, seem to favor the possibility of successful mediation by an outside actor. According to this conditional generalization, a crisis is ripe for mediated resolution when (1) the actors perceive that a deadlock has emerged and fear that things will get worse; (2) they believe that a satisfactory outcome through unilateral action is no longer possible, whereas acceptable joint solutions may be feasible; and (3) the side that previously had the upper hand has slipped and the underdog has gained strength. Zartman characterized such conditions as "a mutually hurting stalemate."[5]

Another example of conditional generalization is provided by a study of the problems that have been encountered in getting the recalcitrant parties in the Arab-Israeli conflict to the negotiating table. Janice Gross Stein analyzed prenegotiation efforts by mediators to achieve this objective in thirteen historical cases. Several conditions were identified that, when present, appeared to favor the success of such efforts:

1.  At least one side must fear a looming crisis, such as the prospect of war.

2.  Both sides must be persuaded that participating in a prenegotiation process is acceptable because the exit costs of failure to agree to go to the table are lower (and more likely to be acceptable) than the exit costs of a failure of direct negotiation.

3.  Both sides must believe that prenegotiation offers the possibility of limiting the scope, participants, and agendas of formal talks that might take place later, thus reducing some of the critical uncertainties and risks of formal negotiation.

4.  One or both sides must believe that participating in prenegotiation will yield useful side effects independent of whether it leads to agreement to enter formal negotiation.[6] The results of both the Zartman and the Stein studies are provisional, subject to refinement or reformulation as additional cases are studied or older cases are reanalyzed.

Other examples of generic knowledge can be cited from the literature on deterrence and coercive diplomacy. Studies of historical cases of failures of deterrence led to the following observation: Deterrence can fail in several ways and for various reasons. One type of deterrence failure occurs when

the adversary attacks in the mistaken belief that no commitment to defend an ally exists. Deterrence can fail even in the
face of such a commitment, however, if the adversary identifies an option for challenging the status quo for which he believes he can calculate and control the risks. (Two such options are the *limited, reversible probe* and the strategy of
*controlled pressure*.) Similarly, studies of the effectiveness of
coercive diplomacy have identified several critically important conditions, all psychological. The success of the strategy
often depends on creating in the opponent's mind (1) a sense
of urgency for compliance with what is demanded, (2) a belief
that asymmetry of motivation favors the coercing power, and
(3) a fear of unacceptable punishment if the demand is not
accepted.[7] These and other conditions that favor coercive diplomacy were discussed in chapter 7. None of the six variables listed in table 7.1 can be regarded as necessary or sufficient conditions for effective coercive diplomacy. But the two
detailed historical case studies that were summarized there
indicate that all six variables played a role: their presence contributed to the success of coercive diplomacy in the Cuban
missile crisis, and their absence contributed to the failure of
coercive diplomacy in the Persian Gulf crisis.

Systematic empirical work is now under way, aimed at producing conditional generalizations with regard to the efficacy
of confidence-building measures. A number of research organizations and investigators are attempting to identify the
conditions that favored the introduction of confidence-building measures in Europe so that they may judge whether similar measures might be adapted for tension-reduction purposes in other regions. The approach taken in a current
project at the Stimson Center in Washington, D.C., supported by the Carnegie Corporation of New York, is particularly noteworthy for making available to policymakers and
policy influentials in a number of countries knowledge of
confidence-building measures that might have relevance to
their own region—a novel way of bringing theory to bear in
practice.[8]

How, then, does generic knowledge of a strategy contribute to policymaking? The favoring conditions for a strategy constitute in effect a checklist that policy analysts can use in diagnosing a problematic situation; the analyst can examine whether the favoring conditions associated with the strategy in past cases are present in the case at hand. However, a diagnosis of this kind cannot be made solely on the basis of available generic knowledge. The policy analyst can judge whether favoring conditions are present only by drawing on available intelligence about the situation and available general knowledge about the adversary; then the analyst can assess how the adversary is likely to respond to the strategy that is being considered.

The reader will ask what level of confidence must be attached to conditional generalizations to make them useful in policymaking. The answer offered here is that conditional generalizations about the efficacy of a strategy do not need the high degree of verification associated with scientific knowledge to remain useful in policymaking. When the level of verification of a generalization is limited or uncertain, the policymaker can still use it responsibly by drawing on available information about the particular case to judge whether the generalization is likely to apply.

Thus, the combined use of generic knowledge of the strategy, intelligence data, and actor-specific knowledge of the particular adversary shapes the policy analyst's diagnosis of the prospects for using the strategy successfully. We turn, therefore, to the third type of knowledge that is relevant for the policymaker's consideration of whether and how to employ a particular strategy in a particular situation against a particular actor.

## Actor-Specific Behavioral Models of Adversaries

To deal effectively with other states, policymakers need what is often referred to as a *correct image* of the opponent. Policy specialists and academic scholars have had no difficulty in agreeing on this fundamental point. They both emphasize that in conducting foreign policy one must try to see events and, indeed, one's own behavior from the perspective of the opponent. Only by doing so can one diagnose a developing situation accurately and select appropriate ways of communicating with and influencing the adversary. Faulty images of each other are a source of misperceptions and miscalculations that have often led to major errors in policy, avoidable catastrophes, and missed opportunities.

When there is little information about an adversary it is common practice to attribute to him a sort of basic and simplified rationality or to see him as a mirror image—someone who calculates the logic of the situation much the same way we do. If in fact the adversary's behavior turns out to be flagrantly and repeatedly at odds with our expectations of a rational actor—that is, if he continues to be hostile despite our efforts to reason with him—then we are tempted to regard him as irrational as well as dangerous. In fact, however, attributing irrationality to an adversary is a questionable way of filling in the vacuum of knowledge about him, just as attributing a basic, oversimplified rationality to him is a questionable substitute for a more refined, differentiated understanding of his values, ideology, culture, and mind-set.

In part two of this study I called attention more than once to questionable aspects of Washington's image of Saddam Hussein and the role it played in the several failed strategies and policies adopted toward Iraq. Many similar examples can be drawn from history. Prior to Nazi Germany's attack on the Soviet Union in 1941, Stalin had ample high-quality intelligence on Hitler's military dispositions and plans. But the Soviet leader did not believe that Hitler would launch a surprise attack, for Stalin's image of the opponent encouraged him to believe that Hitler would present demands and attempt to gain his objectives through bargaining before resorting to force. Stalin therefore misperceived the purpose of the menacing Nazi military buildup on the Soviet border, believing it was intended to set the stage for serious negotiations and coercive bargaining.

An incorrect image of the adversary also played an important role in the Truman administration's mishandling of China's threat to intervene in the Korean War should U.S. forces cross into North Korea and attempt to eliminate the Communist regime. Secretary of State Dean Acheson believed that, since the United States did not harbor aggressive intentions against mainland China, the Chinese leaders should be able to see that their perception of threat was unjustified. Instead of resorting to deterrence or negotiations or both to ward off possible Chinese intervention in Korea, the administration chose the strategy of offering reassurances and invoking the historical friendship between the Chinese and the American peoples.

The importance of the image of the adversary in policymaking is strikingly evident when individual members of a policymaking group operate with different assumptions about the character of the opponent. During the Berlin crisis of 1961, President Kennedy's advisers split into two groups that differed fundamentally on the nature of the Soviet adversary. One group (centered around Dean Acheson, whom the president brought in as a special adviser) operated with the familiar hard-line image of the Soviet Union as an aggressively expansionist power engaged in a long-range, zero-sum conflict with the West. The other group held a somewhat more moderate, nuanced image of the Soviet leaders. To members of this second group it appeared that the expansionist thrust of Soviet foreign policy, if indeed it had been as virulent as feared, was moderating and that Moscow was increasingly operating at times out of nationalist and defensive motives.

Operating as they were with these basically different images of the opponent, the two groups made quite different assessments of the threat posed by Khrushchev's demand for a change in the Berlin situation, and they offered quite differ-

ent recommendations as to how the United States should respond. The essence of the hard-line position was that the Soviets were engaged in an offensive move that posed serious
dangers to the entire western position in Europe. For the
western powers to agree to negotiate or to present an image
of flexibility in the face of Khrushchev's deadline would be to
encourage the Soviets to press for the realization of their far-
reaching objectives. The hard-line group urged a firm response coupling refusal of negotiations with deployment of
additional forces to Europe and a call-up of reserves.

In contrast, and consistent with its more moderate general
image of the Soviet opponent, the other group of advisers
offered a quite different assessment of the threat and a different set of recommendations. They believed that the Soviets
were engaged in an essentially defensive operation in Berlin,
aimed at consolidating their control over Eastern Europe.
Accordingly, these soft-line advisers urged the president to
start negotiations immediately in order to avoid a dangerous
confrontation and also to convey to Moscow a willingness to
reduce the irritants that West Berlin was imposing on Soviet
interests in Eastern Europe. Fearing that the intransigent position advocated by the hard-line school could lead the Soviets to make desperate moves, advocates of the softer line favored immediate negotiations to assure the Soviets that an
effort would be made to meet their legitimate security interests.

In the Cuban missile crisis the image of the opponent
played an important role both in the onset of the crisis and in
its resolution. Khrushchev's defective image of Kennedy—
whom he viewed as a young, inexperienced, weak leader who
could be pushed around and, at the same time, a rational person who would not risk war to get the missiles out—is widely
believed, even by some analysts in the Soviet Union, to have
played a role in his underestimation of the risks of the missile
gambit. On the other hand, Kennedy's correct image of the
Soviet leader—as one who was capable of correcting his mis-

take and withdrawing the missiles if made aware of the risks of refusing to do so—played a role in his choice of the strategy of coercive persuasion rather than military force to remove the missiles. After discovering the missiles in Cuba, U.S. policymakers had to choose between (a) using military action to remove the missiles, and (b) applying coercive diplomatic pressure to persuade Khrushchev to remove them peacefully. Critical to the policy choice was the question whether Khrushchev and his advisers were capable of a diplomatic retreat. Or had the deployment of missiles into Cuba proceeded so far, and were Soviet leaders so committed to the daring venture, that for them there could be no turning back? An answer to this question was suggested by knowledge of an important aspect of the Soviet political style derived from studies of past Soviet behavior and Soviet political doctrine.[9] Readiness to retreat in order to extricate oneself from a situation of overwhelming danger was one of the cardinal maxims of the old Bolshevik doctrine. A good Bolshevik had to know when the time had come for retreat and not let false considerations of pride or emotion get in the way.

In numerous other ways during the Cuban crisis, knowledge of the opponent provided by the State Department specialist on the Soviet Union, Llewellyn Thompson, was of considerable help to Kennedy's advisory group in interpreting Soviet actions and in gauging how Khrushchev and his advisers were likely to react to possible U.S. moves.

In addition to a correct image of the opponent, policymakers need to understand the *adversary's* image of *them*. This variable is often alluded to in emphasizing the importance of trust and of overcoming invidious, distorted stereotypes that disputing parties have of each other. One's self-image, which exercises a subtle influence in shaping one's foreign policy aspirations, goals, and behavior, is seldom the same image that is perceived by the adversary and that influences his perceptions and behavior.

Today there is no disagreement among practitioners and

scholars of foreign policy on the importance of a correct image of the opponent.[10] For a number of years a multidisciplinary group in the Central Intelligence Agency has specialized in developing political-psychological profiles of foreign leaders. Although this work remains classified and an overall assessment of its quality is not possible, it is known that the profiles of Sadat and Begin that were provided to President Carter proved very helpful to him in mediating the Camp David Accords. It has also been reported that Steve Pieczenik, a State Department employee, prepared analyses of Sadat and Begin for the Camp David meeting as well, and that he and Richard Solomon, then head of policy planning at the State Department, developed profiles of Gorbachev for the summit meeting at Reykjavik in 1987 and for discussion about the role that Prince Sihanouk might play in a Cambodian settlement.[11] Similarly, as Llewellyn Thompson's contribution during the Cuban missile crisis indicates, area experts and diplomats have a particularly critical contribution to make to the development of sophisticated images of adversaries.

When one considers what academic scholars can contribute to the development of better behavioral models of actual actors in the international system, several observations come to mind. The rational choice models that some academic scholars favor as an approach to theory development have severe limitations insofar as they attribute to all actors the same generalized rationality. Rational choice theory and applications of game theory fail to contribute to foreign policy decision making when they ignore the policymaker's need for actor-specific models. In other words, the abstract model of rationality has to be supplemented or replaced by an empirically derived theory about the mind-set of a particular actor.

Research is needed that focuses on how a particular actor tends to deal with the various well-known cognitive and political constraints on rationality. Policymakers engaged in strategic interaction with other leaders need behavioral models of the adversary that include information on how decisions are made, who the policy influentials are, and what psychological, cultural, and political variables (which may be quite idiosyncratic) shape and influence that adversary's goals, perceptions, calculations, and behavior. Only area specialists can be expected to provide such specialized models.

* * * *

I have discussed the types of knowledge that can be developed about each of the many undertakings and strategies employed from time to time to further foreign policy objectives in relations with other states. I have also indicated the contribution to policy analysis and policymaking these types of knowledge are capable of making.

Both the development of this knowledge base and its use in policymaking remain quite uneven. These inadequacies were evident in the discussion in part two of strategies the United States employed, mostly without success, in different phases of its relations with Saddam Hussein's Iraq. In employing several of these strategies (resocialization of an outlaw state, appeasement, reassurance, and war termination) policymakers had to operate without a well-developed conceptualization of the task and without generic knowledge of the conditions under which it might succeed. The discussion in part two also called attention to the limitations of the actor-specific model of Saddam Hussein with which U.S. policymakers operated.

The observation that the knowledge base for the strategies we have examined suffers from various inadequacies applies also to many other instruments of statecraft and other foreign policy undertakings. It is true, for example, of knowledge about conflict and dispute resolution techniques. There are exceptions, of course. As already noted, progress has been made in conceptualizing an understanding of the conditions that facilitate getting parties to a dispute to the table. And the concept of "ripeness" of conflicts for mediation has proved to be stimulating and capable of refinement and elaboration as more historical experience is examined from this perspective.

In recent years there has been a great proliferation of strategies for dispute resolution. A recent inventory identified more than twenty-five "programs" and "procedures" for conflict resolution that have been put forward by different specialists. Generally speaking, although the conceptualization of each strategy has been usefully articulated, relatively little systematic empirical research has been done to identify the conditions and processes that lead to successful employment of each of these strategies. Hence, more research will be needed to develop generic knowledge that can help policymakers decide which strategy for dispute resolution is most promising under different conditions.[12]

\* \* \* \*

Before indicating how the three types of knowledge contribute to policy analysis, I need to recall the distinction made in chapter 1 between two basic tasks in policy analysis: (1) diagnosis of the problem situation, and (2) prescription of strategic options for dealing with it. The types of knowledge I have identified contribute first to the *diagnostic* task of policy analysis. This point needs to be emphasized because of a widespread, persistent tendency on the part of scholars to overlook the contribution to diagnosis and to assume that the primary aim of policy-relevant theory and generic knowledge is to contribute to the prescriptive task of policy analysis.

An additional point needs emphasis: the three types of knowledge do not suffice for policy analysis of a problem. Policy analysts must also make use of specific information about that situation provided by intelligence and journalistic sources in order to diagnose it and to prescribe appropriate options for dealing with it.

Finally, the results of policy analysis go to top policymakers who exercise a broader judgment that takes into account the various trade-offs noted earlier as well as other variables and considerations that were either absent or weighted differently in the policy analysis. The job of policy analysts is to provide an *analytic judgment* as to what is likely to be the best policy option. The policymaker, however, has to exercise a broader *political judgment* as to what option is most appropriate or most acceptable in the circumstances. We should also recognize that policymakers need not and often do not wait passively for policy analysts to complete their work and communicate their results. In fact, top policymakers may take the lead in expressing provisional policy preferences and setting boundaries and objectives for policy analysis. Also, there can be considerable discussion back and forth between top policymakers and policy analysts.

Top policymakers themselves sometimes take on major tasks of policy analysis. When they do so without access to or

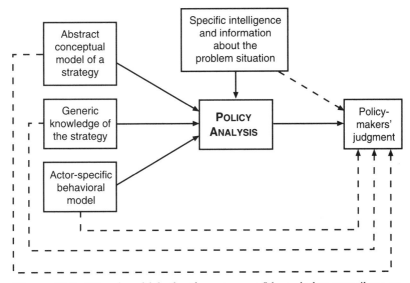

**Figure 10.1.** Ways in which the three types of knowledge contribute to policy analysis.

much use of the types of knowledge we have discussed, we may say that top policymakers substitute their own understanding regarding the strategy in question for the abstract conceptual model of the strategy available to policy specialists, their own assumptions of what conditions favor its success for the available generic knowledge, and their own image of the opponent for the actor-specific behavioral model policy analysts have at their disposal. It is also possible, of course, that top policymakers are already conversant with these types of knowledge or are made conversant with them during the policymaking process.

The contribution of knowledge to policy analysis and to the judgment of top policymakers is depicted in figure 10.1.

# Summary and Conclusions

Scholars specializing in international relations and policy specialists in the government face together the challenging task of improving the knowledge base required for more effective foreign policy. This objective will be furthered by a better understanding of the gap between the theory and practice of foreign policy. Bridging this gap, in turn, requires bridging differences between the two cultures of academia and the policymaking world. Members of these two communities define their interest in international relations somewhat differently; they pursue different professional goals and have difficulty communicating with each other.

However, these differences need not lead to pessimism about the prospects for more effective two-way interaction. Noteworthy is the fact that the boundary between academia and the policymaking arena is quite permeable; there is much movement of individuals across it, and many opportunities exist for joint discussion of policy problems. Individuals who have had experience in both worlds are in a particularly good position to contribute to bridging the gap between scholarly research on international relations and the practice of foreign policy.

As a stratagem for achieving this objective I have suggested that scholars and policy specialists put aside stereotypes of each other and focus instead on their shared interest in better understanding the relationship between knowledge and action. They will find embedded in this relationship three more specific questions that need to be addressed: (1) What kinds of contribution can scholarly knowledge make to policymaking? (2) What types of knowledge are most relevant for policy? (3) How can these types of knowledge be developed by scholars and research specialists, and how can such knowledge be employed in policymaking? Provisional answers to these questions have been provided in this study, but before summarizing them I will restate the major conclusion of chapter 9.

## Broadening the Scope of International Relations Theory

The dominant and most prestigious scholarly theory of international relations is structural realist theory, sometimes called neorealist theory. In chapter 9, I called attention to the limited scope of this theory from the perspective of the knowledge base required for the conduct of foreign policy. Indeed, proponents of structural realism explicitly acknowledge that it is not a theory of foreign policy—although a theory of foreign policy is precisely what policymakers need.

Clearly, scholars who wish to contribute to the development of theory and knowledge that is relevant for the conduct of foreign policy will have to go beyond realist theory. In the present study I have advocated that systematic research be directed toward developing better conceptual and empirical knowledge of each of the many strategies and different types of undertakings that form so much of the substance of foreign policy. Also, I have urged development of more sophisticated actor-specific behavioral models of actors in international politics to replace the simple assumption made by realist theory and other academic approaches that states are rational, unitary actors.

By urging a revival of research on foreign policy strategies

I do not mean to ignore policymakers' need for knowledge about the many substantive problems that affect the security and welfare of the states and peoples of the world and the other kinds of contributions scholars can make (see the Introduction). Rather, given the constraints on what any single study can hope to accomplish, I chose to focus on policymakers' need for better conceptual-empirical knowledge of the uses and limitations of various strategies and instruments of policy.

## Policy-relevant Knowledge

I have identified three types of knowledge that can help policymakers select and implement strategies for influencing adversaries in order to achieve favorable outcomes in interactions with them. These three types of knowledge and the ways they contribute (together with other information) to policymaking are as follows:

*Abstract conceptual models of strategies*

- A conceptual model (or quasi-deductive theory) is not itself a strategy, but it does provide a basic framework for understanding the nature and general requirements for designing an effective strategy.
- The conceptual model identifies the critical variable-components of the strategy to which the policymaker must give specific content.
- The conceptual model also identifies the general logic associated with successful employment of the strategy, but the policymaker must design a variant of the strategy and implement it in ways that will create that logic in the calculations and judgment of the adversary.
- The conceptual model is useful for policymaking even though it remains an incomplete deductive theory and is therefore incapable of predicting specific outcomes.

*Generic knowledge*

- Generic knowledge (i.e., empirical laws and causal patterns) is derived from systematic comparison of explanations of variance in the outcomes of past efforts to make use of a particular strategy.
- Generic knowledge is more useful when it takes the form of conditional generalizations rather than probabilistic generalizations.

*Actor-specific behavioral models*

- Models of this kind are needed to replace the generalized rationality often attributed by policymakers to other actors whose attitudes and behavior they are trying to influence.
- The knowledge and judgment of area specialists is particularly relevant for developing actor-specific models.

Adequate scholarly knowledge of the conceptual and generic types does not yet exist for many of the standard strategies and instruments of policy. And, although there are exceptions, the quality of knowledge of the motivations and behavioral styles of other actors in international politics is uneven and problematic at best.

## Central Themes of the Study

Further progress in bridging the gap between theory and practice requires that scholars take a realistic view of the limited, indirect, and yet important impact that scholarly knowledge about foreign policy can have on policymaking. In addressing this question three central themes were advanced.

First, although the three types of policy-relevant knowledge identified can indeed help bridge the gap, they cannot eliminate it. Rather, scholarly knowledge is best conceptualized as an input to policy analysis of specific issues within the government and as an aid, not a substitute for, the judgments that policymakers must exercise when choosing policies. Chapter 2 identified various types of judgments that policymakers must often make, sometimes at the expense of choosing the policy option that best meets the criterion of analytic rationality.

Second, although scholarly knowledge can generally be expected to make only an indirect, limited contribution to policymaking, its contribution will nevertheless often be critical for the development and choice of sound policies. I demonstrated this point by calling attention in part two to the weak knowledge base undergirding most of the strategies the United States pursued toward Iraq in 1988–91, a defect that contributed to the failure of those policies.

Third, in thinking about the kind of policy-relevant knowledge that needs to be developed we should give more attention to its contribution to the diagnosis of problem situations than to its ability to prescribe sound choices of policy. The three types of knowledge are particularly appropriate for diagnosing situations to which a policy response must be worked out. The same cannot be said for rational choice theories favored by some scholars, for these theories typically bypass the task of situational analysis or deal with it by assumption and instead proceed directly to offering prescriptive advice on policy choices.

## Implications for Scholarly Research and Policymaking

First, it should be recognized that scientific theory and knowledge are not essential for the sensible conduct of foreign policy. Just as intelligent people are generally able to manage the many chores of everyday life reasonably well without benefit of scientific knowledge, so too can intelligent policymakers use the best available "prescientific" knowledge of different aspects of international affairs. To be useful in policymaking, conditional generalizations about the efficacy of a strategy therefore need not satisfy the high degree of verification

associated with scientific knowledge. Of course, ideally policymakers would like the general knowledge on which they
base decisions to have as high a level of verification as possible, but in practice they will settle for more modest levels.
When verification is limited, policymakers can still use conditional generalizations responsibly, even though the generalizations have limited empirical support and therefore are
only plausible.[1] By drawing on available information about a
particular case, policymakers can judge whether the plausible
generalization is likely to hold for that situation.

Second, academic scholars should include in their research
designs variables over which policymakers have some leverage. Strategy is just such a variable. (I referred in chapter
1 to the limited relevance for policymaking of quantitative-
correlational research on international relations that deals
only with non-decision-making variables in attempting to account for variance in foreign policy outcomes.)

Third, taking note of a concern often expressed by policymakers, also identified in chapter 1, scholars should recognize that for their research to be more relevant and useful in
policymaking they should not define concepts and variables
at too high a level of abstraction. The more abstract a concept, the more remote it is from its referent in the real world,
and the greater and more difficult the intellectual demand on
the practitioner to make that linkage and to benefit from it.

Fourth, scholars should recognize that too strict a pursuit
of the scientific criterion of parsimony in their efforts to theorize is inappropriate for developing useful policy-relevant
theory and knowledge. A rich theory—which I define as
one that encompasses a relatively large number of the variables that can influence the outcome of a policy—is often
more useful in policymaking than a simpler theory of narrow
scope, such as structural realist theory, that encompasses only
a few causal variables. The policymaker who has to deal with
complex situations that embrace many variables gets more
help from a rich theory even though it enjoys less verification

than from a simple, parsimonious theory that establishes a linkage of some kind among only a few of the operative variables. This does not mean that the policymaker is reduced to making purely subjective or highly speculative judgments. Thorough verification of rich theories is not a major issue for policymakers since they can try to assess the validity of a theory or generalization for at least the particular case at hand by using the detailed information available on that case.

A rich theory is useful to policymakers if it meets two criteria: its contents must be at least plausible, and it must contain indications of the special conditions under which its propositions are likely to be true or false. Such a rich, differentiated theory serves at the very least as a sophisticated checklist to remind policy analysts and policymakers of the numerous conditions and variables that can influence their ability to achieve desired outcomes and to avoid undesired ones in any given foreign policy activity. When more fully developed, a rich, differentiated theory about a particular type of foreign policy activity identifies those conditions that favor, though they do not guarantee, the policy's success. Such conditions have causal relevance even though they cannot be regarded as either necessary or sufficient conditions for a given outcome to occur.[2]

Fifth, an important objective in developing policy-applicable theory should be to produce just such conditional generalizations. These are more useful in policymaking than generalizations that merely assert a probabilistic relationship between two variables without identifying the conditions under which the relationship does and does not hold. Conditional generalizations are also more useful than deductive theories and universal generalizations that are able to claim no more than perhaps to have identified a necessary condition for the success of a particular policy instrument or undertaking but have nothing to say about what else must also be present for that favorable outcome to occur.

This is not to say, however, that producing conditional

generalizations is a relatively simple research task. For example, despite the considerable research effort of many scholars over the years on the question "Do arms races lead to war?" a recent review of this literature tells us that "there is still no well-developed theory that describes the circumstances under which arms races will or will not lead to war. Nor is there a theory that provides a reliable guide for policymakers."[3] However, increasingly sophisticated research on this question does show that arms races are neither a necessary condition for the occurrence of war (since wars do sometimes occur in the absence of a prior arms race) nor a sufficient condition (since an arms race is not always followed by war). Additional study should result at least in identifying a number of conditions that can be said to favor the likelihood of war and perhaps in identifying ways policymakers can reduce or control the likelihood of an arms race resulting in war.

Sixth, but by no means least in importance, in attempting to develop conditional generalizations scholars should consider whether the phenomenon in question is characterized by *equifinality,* a term from general systems theory that means similar outcomes in different cases of a phenomenon can have different causal explanations. An example of equifinality was the discovery that deterrence can fail in several different ways, leading to the identification of three different causal patterns leading to deterrence failure.[4] Another example of equifinality emerged in the identification of several different paths to "inadvertent war" (a war that occurs even though neither side wanted or expected it at the beginning of the crisis).[5]

The phenomenon of equifinality in fact pervades much of international relations and indeed many other areas of life, as John Stuart Mill recognized so many years ago in his *System of Logic.* Mill warned that the methods of agreement and difference he outlined were not applicable to many social phenomena, because their occurrence was subject to "plurality of causes." Equifinality has important implications not only for the form that causal knowledge of foreign policy outcomes often must take but also for research strategy aimed at developing causal theory. Scholars should not assume, as they often do, that the task of developing theory and causal knowledge consists in finding a single causal generalization for all instances of an undertaking that have resulted in a similar outcome. Rather, the research task will be better pursued and be more fruitful if the investigator is alert to discovering different causal patterns that lead to a similar outcome.

* * * *

In summing up, we may recall from chapter 1 Richard Goodwin's criticism of Schelling's *Arms and Influence*. Goodwin argued that a "systematic theory" of the kind he inferred (incorrectly) that Schelling was proposing is impossible as well as dangerous. The criticism rests on a misunderstanding of systematic theory as something that seeks to provide, or seems to provide, the policymaker with detailed, high-confidence prescriptions for action in each contingency that may arise. Indeed, such a theory does not exist and is not feasible. But the choice is not between (a) detailed, precise, high-confidence prescriptions for action and (b) nothing. Instead of focusing primarily on the prescriptive function of theory I have emphasized as more feasible and useful the contribution that the three types of policy-relevant knowledge identified in this study can make to the diagnosis of specific situations that have to be made before policymakers decide what to do. I also noted the limited but still useful contribution these types of knowledge can make to policy analysis and to decisions on whether to undertake a particular policy and how to design and implement it.

## Implications for the Policymaking Community

This study lends strong support to the observation that top policymakers often operate with inadequate conceptual and generic knowledge of strategies they employ in conducting foreign policy and that such policies are often based on an inaccurate image of the adversary. Not only do these gaps and inadequacies in the knowledge base for foreign policy need to be recognized, but remedial steps need to be taken.

This study also questions the view that policy failures are invariably to be explained by inadequate or faulty intelligence provided to top policymakers and that the remedy lies in improving the quality of intelligence. Such an explanation oversimplifies both the problem and the solution to it. Admittedly, the weak intelligence available on Iraq during the period 1988–91 contributed to the failure of the strategies employed (see chapter 3). But the more fundamental deficiency was the poor conceptualization of several of the strategies and inadequate knowledge of the requirements for making effective use of them.

Only a few brief observations and suggestions will be offered here regarding remedial steps for improving the knowledge base; to go further would require extending the focus of the present study considerably. First, the intelligence community cannot be expected to develop the conceptual and generic knowledge of strategies that policymakers need. The research needed for this purpose requires a particular kind of analytical perspective on foreign affairs and research methods that is more typically possessed by academic scholars than by intelligence specialists. A partial exception is with respect to what I have referred to as actor-specific behavioral models. Important contributions to developing such models can be made by intelligence specialists with area expertise and other qualifications, and by area specialists elsewhere in the government. How well they have done so in the past requires a broader study than the present one. The challenge here is to find ways of making better use of the resources and specialists within the government and drawing more effectively on specialists outside the government. This objective is surely worthy of serious attention within the government.

The development of better conceptual and generic knowledge of strategies is likely to proceed more expeditiously if undertaken by academic scholars who are interested in developing policy-relevant knowledge. Working together or separately, the State Department, the Defense Department, and the National Security Council should devise ways of encouraging scholarly work of this kind at academic centers. At the same time, they should devise procedures for assembling and having ready within the government the best available research on strategies and introducing it on a timely basis into the policymaking process.

# Notes

## Introduction

**1.** For a more detailed statement describing my research program see A. L. George, "Bridging the Gap between Theory and Practice," in James Rosenau (ed.), *In Search of Global Patterns* (New York: Free Press, 1976), pp. 114–119. Discussions of policy-relevant theory appear in A. L. George, D. K. Hall, and W. E. Simons, *Limits of Coercive Diplomacy* (Boston: Little, Brown, 1971), pp. ix–xviii; A. L. George and R. Smoke, *Deterrence in American Foreign Policy; Theory and Practice* (New York: Columbia University Press, 1974), pp. 616–642; R. Smoke and A. L. George, "Theory for Policy in International Relations," *Policy Sciences* (December 1974). My work on "process theory" is summarized in A. L. George, *Presidential Decisionmaking in Foreign Policy: The Effective Use of Information and Advice* (Boulder, CO: Westview Press, 1980). Chapter 6 of that book identifies and illustrates various "malfunctions" of the policy-making process. The problem of evaluating policy decisions is discussed in "Criteria for Evaluation of Decisionmaking," *Global Perspectives*, Vol. 2, No. 1 (Spring 1984): 58–69.

## 1. Academia and Policymaking

**1.** Robert Bowie, as quoted in Ernest R. May (ed.), *Knowing One's Enemies: Intelligence Assessment Before the Two World Wars* (Princeton: Princeton University Press, 1984), pp. 3–4.

**2.** I use the term *practitioners* broadly to include specialists who make different kinds of contributions to the policymaking process.

In addition to top policymakers, they include advisers, policy analysts, intelligence specialists, and functional and area experts. There are important differences in perspective toward scholarly research and its relevance to policymaking between political-level officials (elected or appointed) and career professionals who serve at lower levels in the government. The former are more action-oriented, the latter more likely to give attention to the analysis of policy issues and to be more receptive to the work and views of academic scholars.

3. Carol H. Weiss with Michael J. Bucuvalas, *Social Science Research and Decision-making* (New York: Columbia University Press, 1980), p. 2.

4. For an analysis along similar lines see Robert L. Rothstein, *Planning, Prediction, and Policymaking in Foreign Affairs: Theory and Practice* (Boston: Little, Brown, 1972). Observations similar to some of those in this chapter regarding the "two cultures" are also presented in Daniel Druckman and P. Terrence Hopmann, "Behavioral Aspects of Negotiations on Mutual Security," in P. E. Tetlock et al. (eds.), *Behavior, Society, and Nuclear War*, Vol. 1 (New York: Oxford University Press, 1989), pp. 85–173; Nathan Caplan, Andrea Morrison, and Russell J. Stambaugh, *The Use of Social Science Knowledge in Policy Decisions at the National Level* (Ann Arbor: University of Michigan, 1975); and Weiss with Bucuvalas, *Social Science Research and Decision-making* (see n. 3). See also Harold Guetzkow's report on twenty interviews he conducted with policy specialists in various parts of the government during the summer of 1980 to identify their perceived need for knowledge about alliance behavior. ("Survey of Policy Community" in Michael Don Ward, *Research Gaps in Alliance Dynamics,* Denver: Graduate School of International Studies, University of Denver Monograph Series in World Affairs, 1982, Vol. 19, Book 1, pp. 71–83.)

5. George Ball, "Lawyers and Diplomats," address before the New York Lawyers' Association, New York City, December 13, 1962; Department of State *Bulletin,* December 31, 1962, pp. 987–991.

6. Jerrold M. Post and Raphael Ezekial, "Worlds in Collision: The Uneasy Relationship between the Counter-terroristic Policy Community and the Academic Community, *Terrorism,* Vol. 11.

7. Schelling's book was published by Yale University Press in 1966. Goodwin's review appeared in the *New Yorker,* February 17, 1968.

**8.** Zbigniew Brzezinski, for example, states in his memoir that during his four years as President Carter's national security adviser, he was "very conscious of the degree to which my intellectual arsenal was becoming depleted in the course of a continuous race against time. There was hardly ever any time to think systematically, to reexamine views, or simply to reflect. A broader historical perspective and a sense of direction are the prerequisites for sound policymaking, and both tend gradually to become victims of in-house official doctrine and outlook and of the pressure toward compromise" (*Power and Principle* [New York: Farrar, Straus, Giroux, 1983], p. 514).

**9.** The generic problem, as Ernest May notes (personal communication), is the one that Michael Polanyi diagnosed in his book, *Personal Knowledge* (Chicago: University of Chicago Press, 1974). People have "tacit knowledge" that they have difficulty turning into transferable, explicit knowledge.

**10.** A fuller discussion of conditional generalizations is presented in chapter 9.

**11.** For a detailed analysis of the pitfalls in policymaking from reliance on a single historical analogy and various safeguards see Richard E. Neustadt and Ernest R. May, *Thinking in Time: The Uses of History for Decision-makers* (New York: Free Press, 1986). See also Yaacov Y. I. Vertzberger, "Decisionmakers as Practical-Intuitive Historians: The Use and Abuse of History," in his *The World in Their Minds* (Stanford: Stanford University Press, 1990); Robert Jervis, "How Decisionmakers Learn from History," in his *Perception and Misperception in International Politics* (Princeton: Princeton University Press, 1976); and, on the role that the Korean analogy played in President Johnson's Vietnam decision making, Yuen Foong Khong, *Analogies at War* (Princeton: Princeton University Press, 1992).

**12.** Louis Halle, *American Foreign Policy* (London: G. Allen, 1960), pp. 316, 318. By "philosophically false," Halle probably had in mind the conceptual inadequacy of theories of international relations that ignore or minimize the importance of actors' cognitive beliefs and mind-sets.

## 2. The Role of Knowledge

**1.** For a detailed presentation of process theory, see George, *Presidential Decisionmaking in Foreign Policy* (see Introduction, n. 1).

Chapter 14 discusses the interface between substance and process in policymaking.

**2.** Robert Rothstein provides a useful characterization of "weak theories" that "may be time-bound and value-bound, that provide only tentative and partial explanations of international events, and that necessitate the use of very fallible human judgment in applications" (*The Evolution of Theory in International Relations* [Columbia: University of South Carolina Press, 1991], p. 142).

### 3. Outcomes of U.S. Strategies

**1.** One of these internal papers, "Containing Iraq," was written by Richard Herrmann and Stephen Grummon, both of the Policy Planning Staff, State Department. Another paper, written for president-elect George Bush by Zalmay Khalilzad, also of the Policy Planning Staff, asserted that Iraq had replaced Iran as the more dangerous threat in the region (Don Oberdorfer, "Missed Signals in the Middle East," *Washington Post Magazine*, March 17, 1991; Elaine Sciolino and Michael Wines, *New York Times*, June 27, 1992).

The Khalilzad and Herrmann-Grummon papers were by no means the only internal memoranda produced by policy advisers to the new Bush administration. A different assessment and different advice were contained in a report to the new secretary of state, James Baker, on March 24, 1989, in preparation for his meeting with Iraq's deputy foreign minister. In this report, Paul Hare, acting assistant secretary of state for Near East and South Asia affairs, took note of Iraq's assistance to terrorists, its chemical and biological weapons buildup, its meddling in Lebanon and revival of its border dispute with Kuwait, and its efforts to develop new missiles. Nonetheless, noting the importance of bilateral relations with Iraq—"the strongest state in a region vital to our interests"—Hare urged Baker to strike a conciliatory note and to stress how "pleased" the new administration was that the two countries had become closer, and to note that President Bush had told Saddam Hussein in a message that the United States attaches "great importance to our relations with Iraq." (An account of this recently declassified report is provided by Elaine Sciolino in "1989 Memo to Baker Listed Abuses by Iraq but Urged Conciliation," *New York Times*, September 22, 1992.)

**2.** Oberdorfer, "Missed Signals."

**3.** For detailed accounts of the pre–Gulf War U.S. policy toward Iraq, see, for example, Don Oberdorfer, "Missed Signals"; Elaine

Sciolino, *The Outlaw State* (New York: John Wiley, 1991); Paul A. Gigot, "A Great American Screw-Up; The U.S. and Iraq, 1980–1990," *The National Interest* (Winter 1990–91): 3–10; U.S. News and World Report, *Triumph without Victory: The Unreported History of the Persian Gulf War* (New York: Times Books, Random House, 1992); and the three-part series of articles by Douglass Frantz and Murray Waas in the *Los Angeles Times,* beginning February 23, 1992. See also Richard N. Haass, "One Year after the Gulf War: Prospects for Peace," U.S. Department of State, *Dispatch,* Vol. 3, No. 15.

**4.** *Time* Magazine, October 1, 1990; Oberdorfer, "Missed Signals"; *Washington Post,* July 16, 1991, and May 29, 1992.

**5.** Interview with policy official (April 9, 1992), who stated that, in retrospect, implementation of specific licensing of exports to Iraq had clearly been too lax; oversight and coherence and control over individual export decisions were lacking. On the Deputies Committee policy review see also U.S. News and World Report, *Triumph without Victory,* pp. 18–19.

**6.** As quoted by Oberdorfer, "Missed Signals," p. 36; see also U.S. News and World Report, *Triumph without Victory,* p. 19.

**7.** Testimony by Central Intelligence Agency (CIA) director Robert M. Gates before the House Banking Committee on May 8, 1992, as reported in the *Washington Post,* May 9, 1992. Gates added that by late spring 1990, the CIA had begun to provide information of Iraq's "huge military buildup," but he did not say whether the intelligence estimate of Iraq's intentions was changed before Iraq's invasion of Kuwait in early August.

### 4. Reforming Outlaw States

**1.** Oberdorfer, "Missed Signals"; see also the publications by Paul Gigot, Elaine Sciolino, U.S. News and World Report, and Frantz and Waas (see chap. 3, n. 3). This account of U.S. policy toward Iraq is supported also by interviews of my own with several policy specialists.

**2.** Elaine Sciolino, *New York Times,* May 29, 1992; see also Jeffrey Smith, *Washington Post,* May 29, 1992.

**3.** The foregoing points are from journalistic accounts and analyses that included interviews with policymakers and from a few interviews of my own with policy specialists in the State Department and the staff of the NSC.

**4.** To regard Saddam's response to the VOA broadcast as an emotional overreaction fails to take into account the impact of earlier problems in the U.S.-Iraqi relationship and various U.S. actions that, seen from Saddam's perspective, had gradually strengthened his suspicion that the United States was pursuing a hostile policy aimed at the overthrow of his regime. For a detailed account of the developments before and after Saddam's speech of February 24 that led him to suspect that the United States was participating in a conspiracy to destroy his regime, see, for example, Donald Neff, "The U.S., Iraq, Israel, and Iran: Backdrop to War," *Journal of Palestine Studies*, Vol. 20, No. 4 (Summer 1991): 23–41.

**5.** See, for example, Richard Nisbett and Lee Ross, *Human Inference: Strategies and Shortcomings of Social Judgment* (Englewood Cliffs, NJ: Prentice-Hall, 1985).

**6.** Henry Kissinger, *A World Restored: Europe after Napoleon* (Magnolia, MA: Peter Smith, 1973).

**7.** Yehezkel Dror's *Crazy States* (1971) provides suggestive observations but eschews empirical analysis of past experience. Charles Doran, *The Politics of Assimilation: Hegemony and its Aftermath* (Baltimore: Johns Hopkins Press, 1971), deals with the task of assimilating defeated hegemonic powers back into the international system and should be consulted for hypotheses in studies of the problem of resocializing outlaw states. *Friendly Tyrants*, edited by Daniel Pipes and Adam Garfinkle (1991), deals with the question of whether the United States should (a) attempt to induce authoritarian regimes that cooperate with U.S. security interests to democratize or (b) try to replace such regimes with democratic ones, not with outlaw states that challenge the norms and practices of the international system.

**8.** A former official who was in the government in 1984–85 when the Reagan administration was attempting to coerce Khaddafi into stopping assistance to terrorists recalled in an interview that the administration sent naval forces into the Gulf of Sidra in a deliberate effort to provoke him; the administration hoped to shoot down his planes, thereby humiliating and discrediting him so that he might be ousted. For a detailed account of the Bush administration's last-minute effort before the cease-fire of February 28 to use two specially prepared deep penetration bombs to "get" Saddam in one of his hardened bunkers, see U.S. News and World Report, *Triumph without Victory,* pp. 3–6.

**9.** For a fuller discussion of the nature of GRIT and tit for tat, see A. L. George, P. J. Farley, and A. Dallin (eds.), *U.S.-Soviet Secu-*

*rity Cooperation* (New York: Oxford University Press, 1988), pp. 702–707.

**10.** Robert Axelrod, *Evolution of Cooperation* (New York: Basic Books, 1984).

**11.** Helpful for this purpose would be a list of explicit indicators that the adversary does not accept the norms of the international system and subscribes to and is preparing to achieve the goal of regional or global hegemony. (I am indebted to William Simons for this suggestion.)

**12.** For a more general discussion see Thomas W. Milburn and Daniel J. Christie, "Rewarding in International Politics," *Political Psychology,* Vol. 10, No. 4 (December 1989): 625–645.

**13.** Precisely this objection was raised by members of the National Security Council (NSC) in April 1987 to proposals by Ross Perot that the Reagan administration make conciliatory actions toward North Vietnam to show "good faith," overcome its leaders' distrust of the United States, and thereby encourage Hanoi's cooperation in locating American POWs and MIAs. NSC officials objected on the grounds that such actions would be granting "concessions without performance." In a recent interview one former NSC staff member added, "History has shown that concessions prior to performance is death. They'll take and take. We've learned that over 25 years." Patrick E. Tyler, *New York Times,* July 5, 1992.

**14.** Many writers have analyzed the flaws in the conceptualization of the détente policy and the problems encountered in implementing it. For accounts focusing on aspects of the policy that resembled the reform and resocialization strategies discussed in this chapter, see A. L. George (ed.), *Managing U.S.-Soviet Rivalry* (Boulder, CO: Westview Press, 1983), especially chapters 1, 5, 6, and 13; also A. L. George, "Domestic Constraints on Regime Change in U.S. Foreign Policy: The Need for Policy Legitimacy," in O. R. Holsti, R. M. Siverson, and A. L. George (eds.), *Change in the International System* (Boulder, CO: Westview Press, 1980), 233–262.

**15.** Elaine Sciolino, *New York Times,* June 7, 1992.

## 5. Appeasement

**1.** Evan Luard, "Conciliation and Deterrence: A Comparison of Political Strategies in the Interwar and Postwar Periods," *World Politics* (January 1967).

**2.** Fred C. Iklé, *Every War Must End* (New York: Columbia University Press, 1971), p. 110; J. L. Richardson, "New Perspectives on Appeasement: Some Implications for International Relations," *World Politics,* Vol. 40, No. 3 (April 1988): 312.

**3.** Professor Stephen R. Rock, Vassar College, is doing this study. Drawing on research in progress, Rock presented a paper, "When Appeasement Worked: British Conciliation of the United States, 1895–1905," at the 1988 meeting of the Northeastern Political Science Association. This paper contains a number of general hypotheses, which Rock will assess in studying other cases of successful and abortive appeasement.

**4.** The great European powers made effective use of appeasement in many instances. See, for example, Paul Kennedy, "The Tradition of Appeasement in British Foreign Policy," *British Journal of International Studies,* Vol. 2 (October 1976).

**5.** For a more detailed discussion see G. A. Craig and A. L. George, *Force and Statecraft,* 2d ed. (New York: Oxford University Press, 1990), pp. 134–144, 247–251, 255–257.

**6.** Rock, "When Appeasement Worked," pp. 19–20 (see n. 3).

**7.** Barbara Tuchman, *The March of Folly* (New York: Knopf, 1984), chap. 4; cited in Rock, "When Appeasement Worked," p. 17. A related, fifth scenario is suggested by Stephen Stedman (in a personal communication): a situation in which appeasement might have succeeded at an early stage in the dispute but became more difficult because reliance on deterrence or force hardened the adversary's position.

**8.** Craig and George, *Force and Statecraft,* p. 254; see also pp. 93–99.

**9.** Craig and George, *Force and Statecraft,* pp. 257–260.

**10.** See, for example, Rock, "When Appeasement Worked"; Kennedy, "The Tradition of Appeasement in British Foreign Policy"; and Charalambos Papasatiriou, *Grand Strategy of the Byzantine Empire,* Ph.D. dissertation, Department of Political Science, Stanford University, 1991.

## 6. Deterrence and Reassurance

**1.** Useful accounts and interpretations appear in a number of published sources, including various contemporary journalistic reports not cited here; see, for example, Oberdorfer, "Missed Signals," and Sciolino, *The Outlaw State* (see chap. 3, n. 3). A particularly well-documented and incisive analysis is provided by Janice

Gross Stein, "Deterrence and Compellance in the Gulf, 1990–1991: A Failed or Impossible Task?" *International Security*, Vol. 17, No. 2 (Fall 1992): 147–179.

**2.** Another strategy for testing and challenging deterrence is available when the challenger (a) believes that the defender's deterrence commitment is soft and may be eroded under carefully controlled pressure, or (b) believes he has a way of bypassing the defender's commitment by trying to change the situation in ways the defender cannot respond to effectively. This is the "controlled pressure" strategy. On the other hand, when the challenger is not sure whether a deterrence commitment exists he can "test" to find out by a "limited probe" strategy that can be terminated if the defender responds by making it clear he does have a commitment and will fight. For detailed discussion and historical examples of these two strategies see George and Smoke, *Deterrence in American Foreign Policy*, chap. 18 (see Introduction, n. 1).

**3.** Quoted in Elaine Sciolino with Michael Gordon, *Washington Post*, September 23, 1990.

**4.** For an account of the Truman administration's erroneous assessment of Chinese intentions and its gross mishandling of the Chinese threat to intervene in the Korean War see, for example, George and Smoke, *Deterrence in American Foreign Policy*, pp. 184–234 (see Introduction, n. 1); see also Allen Whiting, "The U.S.-China War in Korea," in A. L. George (ed.), *Avoiding War: Problems of Crisis Management* (Boulder, CO: Westview Press, 1991), pp. 103–125. Whiting's chapter updates with new material on U.S. and Chinese decisionmaking his earlier classic study, *China Crosses the Yalu* (Stanford: Stanford University Press, 1968).

**5.** These interpretations of Mao's thinking, advanced many years ago by scholars (see Whiting, *China Crosses the Yalu*), are supported by the recent publication of a secret cable from Mao to Stalin on October 2, 1950 (*New York Times*, February 26, 1992).

**6.** The best discussion of various reassurance strategies that may be adopted instead of or in conjunction with deterrence is Janice Gross Stein's "Deterrence and Reassurance," in Philip E. Tetlock et al., *Behavior, Society, and Nuclear War* (New York: Oxford University Press, 1991), Vol. 2, pp. 8–72. See also the earlier article by Janice Gross Stein, "Reassurance in International Conflict Management," *Politcial Science Quarterly*, Vol. 106, No. 3 (Fall 1991): 431–451, and the one by Richard Ned Lebow and Janice Gross Stein, "Beyond Deterrence," *Journal of Social Issues*, Vol. 43, No. 4 (1987): 5–71.

**7.** In this connection Stein argues in a recent paper ("Deterrence and Compellance"; see n. 1) that Saddam Hussein was convinced that the United States was masterminding a plot against his regime and, therefore, that it would have been very difficult, if not impossible, for the United States to devise a strategy of reassurance that could have altered his decision to attack Kuwait. Stein also calls attention to the weakness of the reassurances that Washington conveyed, which did not address the economic difficulties and needs, driven in part by his expensive military programs, that Saddam began voicing with increasing urgency in the spring of 1990. Nor does it appear that Washington urged the Kuwaiti government to be more forthcoming in dealing with Saddam's demands. According to another interpretation of Saddam Hussein's decision to invade Kuwait, he did so largely as a result of acute economic difficulties and the prospect that without a massive increment of new money he would be unable to afford the level of spending needed to maintain the momentum of his massive weapons program. A similar interpretation of Saddam's image of a fundamentally hostile United States is given in Paul K. Davis and John Arquilla, *Deterring or Coercing Opponents in Crisis: Lessons from the War with Saddam Hussein* (Santa Monica, CA: The RAND Corporation, 1991).

### 7. Failure to Coerce Saddam

**1.** The most satisfactory analytical study of why the administration moved from sanctions to the threat of war and why the ultimatum failed is Richard K. Herrmann, "Coercive Diplomacy and the Crisis over Kuwait: 1990–1992," in A. L. George (ed.), *The Limits of Coercive Diplomacy*, 2d ed. (forthcoming). Important insights and interpretations are to be found in Shibley Telhami, "Between Theory and Fact: Explaining American Behavior in the Gulf War," unpublished manuscript, 1992.

**2.** The information presented here is provisional and somewhat speculative, yet informed by an interview with a senior policy specialist who participated in the working group's activities.

**3.** According to Bob Woodward, the CIA issued a special pre-Christmas national intelligence estimate that concluded that Saddam would pull out once he realized the size of the force arrayed against him. On the other hand, a Defense Intelligence Agency specialist, Pat Lang, suspected the opposite. In mid-December Gen. Colin Powell thought that Saddam would withdraw from Kuwait at the last minute, but Secretary (of Defense) Dick Cheney disagreed.

National security adviser Brent Scowcroft did not believe the ultimatum would work and that war would be necessary. In an interview with *Time* magazine shortly before Christmas, President Bush was asked if there would be war and responded, "My gut says he will get out of there" (Bob Woodward, *The Commanders* [New York: Simon and Schuster, 1991], pp. 274, 345, 351, 354–5). Woodward adds (p. 358) that in a meeting with President Bush and other policymakers on January 8, ambassador to Iraq April Glaspie expressed the belief that Saddam would not withdraw from Kuwait. And the head of policy planning in the State Department believed that Saddam would agree to pull out of Kuwait at the last minute.

**4.** Jerrold M. Post, "Saddam Hussein of Iraq: A Political Psychology Profile," *Political Psychology*, Vol. 12, No. 2 (June 1991). An earlier version of the paper began circulating widely in Washington in September 1990 and was the basis for Dr. Post's testimony before the hearings on the Gulf crisis held by the House Armed Services Committee on December 5 and the House Foreign Affairs Committee on December 12. A similar image of Saddam—held by Dennis Ross, head of policy planning in the State Department—is described later in this chapter.

**5.** David Hoffman, *Washington Post,* October 28, 1991.

**6.** Jerrold M. Post, "Afterword," *Political Psychology*, Vol. 12, No. 4 (1992): 723–725.

**7.** For additional analysis of the uses and limitations of coercive diplomacy and a comparative study of seven cases in which the United States has used this strategy, see A. L. George, *Forceful Persuasion: Coercive Diplomacy as an Alternative to War* (Washington, DC: United States Institute of Peace Press, 1991).

## 8. War Termination

**1.** For useful summaries and discussion of the literature on war termination see Janice Gross Stein, "War Termination and Conflict Reduction or, How Wars Should End," in *Jerusalem Journal of International Relations*, Vol. 1, No. 1 (Fall 1975): 1–27; and William T. R. Fox (ed.), special issue on war termination, *Annals of the American Academy of Political and Social Science*, Vol. 392 (November 1970).

**2.** An oddity of the Gulf War is that U.S. policy aimed at the elimination of Saddam Hussein added an objective characteristic of total war to what was otherwise a limited war.

**3.** See, for example, *Newsweek,* March 11, April 1, and April 8, 1992.

**4.** U.S. News and World Report, *Triumph without Victory,* pp. 3–6 (see chap. 3, n. 3).

**5.** A detailed account of the decision to declare a cease-fire before the envelopment of the Iraqi troops in the Basra area was completed is given in U.S. News and World Report, *Triumph without Victory,* pp. 308–398 and 399–403. Important details are provided in General H. Norman Schwarzkopf's *It Doesn't Take a Hero* (New York: Linda Grey/Bantam Books, 1992), pp. 468–472.

**6.** According to Bob Woodward, *The Commanders* (see chap. 7, n. 3), General Powell conveyed to General Schwarzkopf the need for restraint in inflicting damage on Iraq: "Powell was convinced that it would not be in the U.S. interest to have a totally defeated Iraq with no capability to defend itself" (p. 374). See also *Newsweek,* April 22, 1991: "Indeed, the United States intentionally refrained from destroying the entire Iraq Army . . . so that enough soldiers would be left to topple the dictator and hold the country together. Under new and stable leadership, the theory went, Iraq would not disintegrate into another Lebanon."

**7.** *Newsweek,* April 22, 1991.

**8.** General Schwarzkopf also minimizes the importance of the Iraqi helicopter gunships: "The tanks and artillery of the twenty-four Iraqi divisions that never entered the Kuwaiti war zone were having a far more devastating effect on the insurgents [than the Iraqi helicopters]" (*It Doesn't Take a Hero,* p. 489).

**9.** General Schwarzkopf, on the other hand, states in his book that "the option of going all the way to Baghdad was never considered" (*It Doesn't Take a Hero,* p. 497). What he apparently means is that choosing this option was not seriously considered, and he summarizes the various reasons for not attempting to seize Baghdad.

**10.** In this connection, it has been suggested that the administration's reluctance to support the Shi'ites in southern Iraq stemmed in part from a misplaced concern that they were like the Shi'ites in Iran.

### 9. Contemporary International Relations Theory

**1.** For a good discussion of why prediction is so difficult in international relations, see Robert Jervis, "The Future of World Politics: Will It Resemble the Past?" *International Security,* Vol. 16, No. 3 (Winter 1991–92): 39–73.

**2.** For a commentary on the Third Debate now in progress see, for example, Yale H. Ferguson and Richard W. Mansback, "Between Celebration and Despair: Constructive Suggestions for Future International Theory," *International Studies Quarterly*, Vol. 35, No. 4 (December 1991): 363–386.

**3.** For useful analytical commentaries on the state of research on international relations see Ole R. Holsti, "Models of International Relations and Foreign Policy," *Diplomatic History*, Vol. 13, No. 1 (Winter 1989): 15–43; and Stephen M. Walt, "The Renaissance of Security Studies," *International Studies Quarterly*, Vol. 35 (1991): 211–239.

**4.** Kenneth Waltz, *Theory of International Politics* (New York: McGraw-Hill, 1979). Waltz provides an interesting account of his reservations about classical realist theory in his "Realist Thought and Neorealist Theory," in Robert L. Rothstein (ed.), *The Evolution of Theory in International Relations* (University of South Carolina Press, 1991), pp. 21–39.

**5.** For an incisive discussion see Robert O. Keohane, "Realism, Neorealism, and the Study of World Politics," in Keohane (ed.), *Neorealism and Its Critics* (New York: Columbia University Press, 1986). There are a number of other critical evaluations of the realist paradigm. See, for example, John A. Vasquez, *The Power of Power Politics: A Critique* (New Brunswick, NJ: Rutgers University Press, 1983).

**6.** For an example of a full-fledged deductive theory, one that operationalizes key variables, see Bruce Bueno de Mesquita, *The War Trap* (New Haven: Yale University Press, 1981), which does generate preductions for each of a large number of specific historical cases. This study is unusual and, whatever reservations one may have about the implementation and results, is particularly valuable for its explicit specification of what is required to operationalize a deductive theory.

**7.** Waltz, *Theory of International Politics*, pp. 121–122.

**8.** See, for example, Vinod K. Aggarwal, *Liberal Protectionism: The International Politics of Organized Textile Trade* (Berkeley: University of California Press, 1985); and David B. Yoffie, *Power and Protectionism: Strategies of the Newly Industrialized Countries* (New York: Columbia University Press, 1983). See also Robert Keohane, "The Big Influence of Small Allies," *Foreign Affairs*, No. 2 (1971): 161–182. My initial formulation of the distinction between gross capabilities and usable options appeared in George et al., *Limits of Coercive Diplomacy*, p. 8 (see Introduction, n. 1).

**10. Types of Knowledge**

**1.** Charles Hitch, one of the founders of modern systems analysis, emphasized many years ago that the results of even the best systems analysis study should be regarded as an aid to the preparation of policy decisions and not a substitute for the judgment of the policymaker.

**2.** Quite unusual in the scholarly literature on international conflict is the operationalized deductive theory of war initiation decisions presented in Bruce Bueno de Mesquita, *The War Trap* (New Haven: Yale University Press, 1981). The author substitutes for the general assumption of rational decision making a more refined concept of "positive utility," which he operationalizes. However, the resulting deductive theory does not predict war initiation but, rather, merely that positive utility will be present if war is initiated. Accordingly, although advancing the general claim that he has produced a theory of the causes of war, the author qualifies it substantially by conceding that positive utility is a necessary but not a sufficient condition for war initiation. Since there are numerous cases in which positive utility was present but the actor did not initiate war, positive utility cannot be regarded as a sufficient condition for war initiation. There are also numerous cases in the study in which war was initiated in the absence of positive utility, which calls into question whether it can be regarded as a necessary condition for war initiation. The question has been raised whether the occurrence of war, versus the initiation of war by one side, can be adequately studied by focusing exclusively on one actor's decision making. A theory of war seems to require the development of two-sided strategic interaction models. Even such models would have to contend with the familiar observation that the outcomes of strategic interactions are indeterminate.

**3.** For a description of the historical explanation method see A. L. George, "Case Studies and Theory Development: The Method of Structured, Focused Comparison," in Paul Gordon Lauren (ed.), *Diplomacy: New Approaches in History, Theory, and Policy* (New York: Free Press, 1979), pp. 43–68.

**4.** George Downs, "Arms Races and War," in Philip E. Tetlock et al. (eds.), *Behavior, Society, and Nuclear War* (New York: Oxford University Press, 1991), Vol. 2.

**5.** I. William Zartman, *Ripe for Resolution: Conflict and Intervention in Africa* (New York: Oxford University Press, 1985). Several years later, applying Zartman's theory of ripeness to a study of several efforts to mediate the civil war in Rhodesia, Stephen Stedman offered several refinements and amendments to the theory in *Peacemaking in Civil War: International Mediation in Zimbabwe, 1974–1980* (Boulder, CO: Lynne Rienner, 1991). More recently, Zartman addressed the question whether the concept of "ripeness," as he initially formulated it, is too culturally determined and needs to be reformulated to encompass variations. See I. William Zartman, "Beyond the Hurting Stalemate" (Paper presented at the Thirty-third Annual Convention, International Studies Association, Atlanta, March 31 to April 4, 1992). On "ripeness" see also Richard N. Haass, *Conflicts Unending: the United States and Regional Disputes* (New Haven: Yale University Press, 1990).

**6.** Janice Gross Stein (ed.), *Getting to the Table: The Process of International Prenegotiation* (Baltimore: Johns Hopkins Press, 1989); and, particularly, an unpublished draft paper by Stein, "The Negotiating Table: Foreground and Background" (prepared for the United States Institute of Peace), which the author has kindly allowed me to see.

**7.** For a detailed discussion see George and Smoke, *Deterrence in American Foreign Policy* (see Introduction, n. 1); and George, *Forceful Persuasion* (see chap. 7, n. 7).

**8.** For example, Cathleen S. Fisher, "The Preconditions of Confidence-Building: Lessons from the European Experience" (unpublished manuscript, 1992); and Alan Platt (ed.), *Arms Control and Confidence Building in the Middle East* (Washington, DC: United States Institute of Peace Press, 1992).

**9.** See, for example, the writings of George Kennan and Nathan C. Leites, *A Study of Bolshevism* (Glencoe, Ill.: Free Press, 1953).

**10.** This point is emphasized and some of the components of an actor-specific behavioral model are identified in Richard Herrmann's current writings. See, for example, "Policy-Relevant Theory and the Challenge of Diagnosis: the End of the Cold War as a Case Study" (unpublished manuscript, 1992). See also James N. Rosenau's call for the development of "single-country" theories in "Toward Single-Country Theories of Foreign Policy: The Case of the USSR," in C. F. Hermann, C. W. Kegley, Jr., and J. R. Rosenau (eds.), *New Directions in the Study of Foreign Policy* (Boston: Allen & Unwin, 1987), pp. 53–74.

**11.** Richard H. Solomon, "Political Culture and Diplomacy in the Twenty-first Century," in Richard J. Samuels and Myron Weiner (eds.), *The Political Culture of Foreign Area and International Studies* (Washington, DC: Brassey's [US], 1992), p. 147.

**12.** Lynn Wagner has produced an extremely useful inventory and discussion of the defining characteristics of each of these strategies in "Processes for Impasse Resolution," working paper 91–43 (Laxenburg, Austria: International Institute for Applied Systems Analysis, December 1991).

## Summary and Conclusions

**1.** A conditional generalization is "plausible" if it is not contradicted by available evidence and if at least some evidence supports it. For a detailed discussion of the limits of scientific verification in social science and the need to settle for degrees of "acceptable" verification, see chapter 10 in Charles E. Lindblom, *Inquiry and Change: The Troubled Attempt to Understand and Shape Society* (New Haven, CT: Yale University Press, 1990).

**2.** For a fuller statement and illustration of this point see George et al., *Limits of Coercive Diplomacy,* p. xvi (see Introduction, n. 1); and George, "Case Studies and Theory Development," pp. 59–60 (see chap. 10, n. 3).

**3.** Downs, "Arms Races and War," p. 75 (see chap. 10, n. 4).

**4.** George and Smoke, *Deterrence in American Foreign Policy* (see Introduction, n. 1).

**5.** George (ed.), *Avoiding War* (see chap. 6, n. 4).

# Index

Realist theory (*cont.*)
  neorealist theory vs. classical,
    108–109
Reassurance strategies, 43, 77–78,
  102
Research. *See also* Scholars/scholar-
    ship
  developing conditional general-
    izations, 120, 122
  empirical vs. deductive, xxi
  flawed data in, 10
  ideological bias in, 10
  integration with practice, 3–6,
    16–17, 135–136
  practitioner views of, 7
  quantitative, in foreign policy, 8
Resocialization, strategies for. *See
    also* Conditional reciprocity
  comparative analysis, 57
  complications in, 56–57
  conceptualizations of, 5, 43,
    101–102
  Iraq, basis for applying, 45–48
  Nazi Germany, 59
  Nixon-Kissinger détente strat-
    egy, 56, 57–59
  outlaw states, 49–50
  prisoners' dilemma, 53–54
  targeted at Saddam Hussein,
    34–35, 36, 37, 40
Resources
  allocating, in policymaking pro-
    cess, 22–24
  relative strengths of conflicting
    states, 109–112
Revolutionary states, 48
Rewards. *See also* Conditional reci-
    procity
  behavior modification via, 55
  bribes vs., 52
  timing of, 55–56
Rock, Stephen, 68
Ross, Dennis, 84

Sadat, Anwar, 30
Saddam Hussein. *See also* Gulf
    War; Iraq

anti-U.S. rhetoric, 37, 47–48
  failure of ultimatum against, 84
  ouster of, efforts at, 39, 91–92,
    94–95, 97–99
  perception of U.S. policy, 72–73,
    77–78
  psychological study of, 83, 84–
    86, 126
  seen as reformable, 34–35, 36,
    37, 40, 45, 74
  seen as susceptible to threat,
    82–83
  threats against Kuwait, 71
Saudi Arabia, 38, 72, 73, 82
Schelling, Thomas, 10–11, 17, 143
Scholars/scholarship
  analytic rationality, 7
  integration with policymaking,
    3–6, 16–17, 135–136
  international relations theory,
    107–108
  language of, 7, 140
  practitioners' traditional views
    of, 6–11
  professional culture of, 15–16
  role of, xix–xx, xxiii, xxiv, 9,
    19–20, 21, 28–29, 116,
    130–131, 132–134, 136–
    137, 138–145
  and trade-off dilemmas, 24–25
  traditional approach to foreign
    policy, 3–4
  traditional views of foreign pol-
    icy practice, 11–15
  understanding practitioner
    needs, 16
Science
  foreign policy as, 8, 22
  psychological, 9–10
Scowcroft, Brent, 36
Security issues, substantive theory
    in research on, xxii
Shi'ite rebellion, 90, 92, 93–94,
    97–98, 99
Sihanouk, Norodom, 130
Solomon, Richard, 130
South Korea, 73

# United States Institute of Peace

The United States Institute of Peace is an independent, nonpartisan federal institution created and funded by Congress to strengthen the nation's capacity to promote the peaceful resolution of international conflict. Established in 1984, the Institute meets its congressional mandate through an array of programs, including grants, fellowships, conferences and study groups, library services, publications, and other educational activities. The Institute's Board of Directors is appointed by the President of the United States and confirmed by the Senate.

**Board of Directors**

**Chester A. Crocker** (Chairman), Distinguished Research Professor of Diplomacy, School of Foreign Service, Georgetown University

**Max M. Kampelman,** Esq. (Vice Chairman), Fried, Frank, Harris, Shriver and Jacobson, Washington

**Dennis L. Bark,** Senior Fellow, Hoover Institution on War, Revolution, and Peace, Stanford University

**Thomas E. Harvey,** Senior Vice President and General Counsel, Corporation for Public Broadcasting

**Theodore M. Hesburgh,** President Emeritus, University of Notre Dame

**William R. Kintner,** Professor Emeritus of Political Science, University of Pennsylvania

**Christopher H. Phillips,** former U.S. Ambassador to Brunei

**Elspeth Davies Rostow,** Stiles Professor of American Studies Emerita, Lyndon B. Johnson School of Public Affairs, University of Texas

**Mary Louise Smith,** civic leader; former member, Board of Directors, Iowa Peace Institute

**W. Scott Thompson,** Professor of International Politics, Fletcher School of Law and Diplomacy, Tufts University

**Allen Weinstein,** President, Center for Democracy, Washington

*Members ex officio*

**Paul G. Cerjan,** Lieutenant General, U.S. Army, and President, National Defense University

**Stephen J. Hadley,** Assistant Secretary of Defense for International Security Policy

**Ronald F. Lehman II,** Director, U.S. Arms Control and Disarmament Agency

**Melvyn Levitsky,** Assistant Secretary of State for International Narcotics Matters

**Samuel W. Lewis,** President, United States Institute of Peace (nonvoting)

# Jennings Randolph Program for International Peace

As part of the statute establishing the United States Institute of Peace, Congress envisioned a fellowship program that would appoint "scholars and leaders of peace from the United States and abroad to pursue scholarly inquiry and other appropriate forms of communication on international peace and conflict resolution." The program was named after Senator Jennings Randolph of West Virginia, whose efforts over four decades helped to establish the Institute.

Since it began in 1987, the Jennings Randolph Program has played a key role in the Institute's effort to build a national center of research, dialogue, and education on critical problems of conflict and peace. Through a rigorous annual competition, outstanding men and women from diverse nations and fields are selected to carry out projects designed to expand and disseminate knowledge on violent international conflict and the wide range of ways it can be peacefully managed or resolved.

The Institute's Distinguished Fellows and Peace Fellows are individuals from a wide variety of academic and other professional backgrounds who work at the Institute on research and education projects they have proposed and participate in the Institute's collegial and public outreach activities. The Institute's Peace Scholars are doctoral candidates at American universities who are working on their dissertations.

Institute fellows and scholars have worked on such varied subjects as international negotiation, regional security arrangements, conflict resolution techniques, international legal systems, ethnic and religious conflict, arms control, and the protection of human rights, and these issues have been examined in settings throughout the world.

As part of its effort to disseminate original and useful analyses of peace and conflict to policymakers and the public, the Institute publishes book manuscripts and other written products that result from the fellowship work and meet the Institute's high standards of quality.

Michael S. Lund
Director